ANTICIPATING HIS ARRIVAL

A Family Guide through Advent

ANTICIPATING HIS ARRIVAL

A Family Guide through Advent

Rick Brannan

LEXHAM PRESS

For Amy, Ella, Lucas, and #3

Anticipating His Arrival: A Family Guide through Advent

Copyright 2015 Lexham Press
Print edition copyright 2016 Lexham Press

Lexham Press, 1313 Commercial St., Bellingham, WA 98225
LexhamPress.com

Print ISBN 9781577996903
Digital ISBN 9781577996910

Lexham Editorial: Abby Salinger, Abigail Stocker
Cover Design: Christine Gerhart
Typesetting: ProjectLuz.com

CONTENTS

FOREWORD

When I was growing up, Advent was a part of celebrating the Christmas season. In my adult life, when I began to worship at a nondenominational community church, Advent was not observed or mentioned at all. And I missed it.

A few years later, my wife and I became involved in a new church plant, and I decided to write a short devotional for Advent for church families to use. The church even printed a limited run, and it was well received.

I used one year of the reading schedule from the Revised Common Lectionary (RCL) as the basis for the readings. If you know anything about the RCL, you probably know it is based on a three-year cycle. So in the years following my original work, I wrote (and rewrote) devotional material for each year of the lectionary cycle. The devotional now has readings for each liturgical year and can be used perpetually with the standard church calendar.

I'm grateful to Lexham Press for wanting to publish this little book, which has been so useful and encouraging to my own family and the families of friends.

My family's prayer is that during the Advent season, you and yours will be drawn into the wonder of the Messiah—God become human—and begin to look forward to his second coming. We pray that this Advent, you will anticipate his arrival.

Rick Brannan
August 2015

INTRODUCTION

Advent is observed each of the four Sundays before Christmas. In the church I grew up in, which did not follow the liturgical calendar, we still observed Advent using a wreath with five candles: four purple candles on the wreath itself, with a white candle in the middle. On each of the four Sundays before Christmas, a purple candle was lit in conjunction with a Scripture reading. There was also a Scripture reading on the Christmas Day service, with the white candle lit on that day. For me, Advent signaled that Christmas was coming—and that Christmas was about much more than giving and receiving presents.

This devotional provides Scripture readings for each week and each day of the Advent season. Questions and responses for each reading are supplied. These can be used for reading and meditation or to start a discussion in a family context.

Use of the Revised Common Lectionary
Weekly readings in this devotional come from the Revised Common Lectionary (RCL).[1] The readings are spread out

---

1. Consultation on Common Texts, *Revised Common Lectionary* (Bellingham, WA: Logos Research Systems, Inc., 2009). The lectionary has a three-year cycle, with years labeled A, B, and C. This devotional includes each liturgical year. Year A begins on November 27, 2016; Year B begins on December 3, 2017; and Year C begins on December 2, 2018.

across each week of Advent, providing daily readings for the entire Advent season.

The RCL is based on a three-year cycle of weekly readings, with each year given a letter (A, B, and C). The lectionary is based on the liturgical year, which begins with the season of Advent. Each liturgical year (A, B, and C) is represented in this devotional, providing a three-year cycle for family Advent reading.

Each liturgical year has a different weekly reading schedule, and each year places one of the Synoptic Gospels into focus. In this scheme, year A focuses on Matthew, year B focuses on Mark, and year C focuses on Luke.

This devotional spreads the weekly readings of the RCL across each week of Advent. This provides a reading for each day of the Advent season, from the first Sunday of Advent (typically the Sunday after Thanksgiving in the U.S.) through Christmas Day.

Basic Design

Each week of Advent focuses on a theme:

> **Week 1:** Preparation
>
> **Week 2:** Anticipation
>
> **Week 3:** Joy
>
> **Week 4:** Incarnation

Each day's reading has a series of questions and responses that focus on the day's passage in light of the week's theme.

Discussion Questions

As noted above, each daily reading also lists questions and responses. These questions and responses do not originate with the lectionary—rather, I have added them to this devotional to provide a starting point for individual reflection or family discussions during the Advent season. The questions are intended as discussion starters. The responses are not intended to be the end of the discussion, but to act as guidelines in the context of family devotions. Please use these questions and responses however you see fit in the context of your personal or family devotions.

The discussion questions section ends with the same question for each daily reading. The purpose of repeating the question is to consider the theme for the week in light of the reading for the day.

Suggested Use

Keeping a family devotional time is difficult, and consistently preparing for that time is sometimes the most difficult part. In the midst of the busyness of the holiday season, family devotions can be even more difficult to maintain. This Advent devotional guide can help you prepare. The design and intent is for simple, short readings with simple, short questions to provoke discussion or thought.

Use of this devotional can be as simple as pulling the guide out after dinner and reading the Scriptures for the day, or using it as a nighttime devotional before putting the kids to bed. Questions and responses are provided so that no preparation is necessary: Just read the questions and discuss, referring to the responses as necessary.

Christmas Eve and Christmas Day

Each of the four weeks of Advent has readings assigned for every day of the week (Sunday through Saturday). Each year, however, Christmas Eve and Christmas Day fall on different days of the week. Because of this, separate readings are provided for Christmas Eve and Christmas Day. The intent is not for two readings on those days. On Christmas Eve, feel free to skip the scheduled daily reading and use the Christmas Eve reading; and feel free to do the same for Christmas Day.

In this way, this devotional can be used for any season of Advent, and perhaps this devotional can even become part of your family's Advent tradition.

On the Use of "Yahweh"

In the Hebrew Bible, one of the names of God is Yahweh. English translations of the Hebrew Bible handle this several different ways. Some older Bibles have "Jehovah"; many newer Bibles use LORD (in small capital letters). This devotional uses the Lexham English Bible (LEB) as its primary text. When possible, the LEB translates the Hebrew as "Yahweh." Questions and responses in this devotional use Yahweh, in reference to the text of the LEB.

YEAR A
ADVENT READINGS

Year A of the three-year liturgical cycle focuses on Matthew for its gospel readings, which form the basis of each week's readings for Advent. A reading from Matthew 24 about the Son of Man calls us to prepare for the second Advent. The discussion in Matthew 3 of John the Baptist leads us—like John—to anticipate the coming of the Messiah. The interaction in Matthew 11 between John the Baptist's disciples and Jesus opens our eyes to Jesus as long-awaited Messiah, bringing us joy. And the story of the first Advent in Matthew 1 reminds us of the wonder that is the incarnation.

WEEK ONE: Preparation

In this first week of Advent, our goal is to set our minds on what is coming. Remembering and considering prophecies about Christ's second coming is about preparing our minds and our thinking—about setting our minds on what is above. But preparation also involves action. If we are preparing for a hurricane, we don't only watch weather reports to verify that we are in its path—we also prepare the house, store supplies, and create an evacuation plan.

Preparation for the coming of Christ means remembering what we have been told about his coming and actively preparing for his arrival.

SUNDAY: Isaiah 2:1-5

The word that Isaiah son of Amoz saw concerning Judah and Jerusalem:

And it shall happen in the future of the days
the mountain of the house of Yahweh shall be established;
it will be among the highest of the mountains,
    and it shall be raised from the hills.
All of the nations shall travel to him;
    many peoples shall come.
And they shall say,

"Come, let us go up to the mountain of Yahweh,
    to the house of the God of Jacob,
and may he teach us part of his ways,
    and let us walk in his paths."
For instruction shall go out from Zion,
    and the word of Yahweh from Jerusalem.
He shall judge between the nations
    and he shall arbitrate for many peoples.
They shall beat their swords into ploughshares
    and their spears into pruning hooks.
A nation shall not lift up a sword against a nation,
    and they shall not learn war again.

House of Jacob, come and let us walk in the light
of Yahweh.

Discussion Questions

1. Isaiah is relating a prophecy. What is a prophecy?

   Response: A prophet speaks the word of the Lord to the Lord's people. As a prophet, Isaiah was responsible for relaying what the Lord told him to the people. So a prophecy is the message the prophet delivers to the Lord's people.

2. What prophecy is Isaiah relating? What will happen?

   Response: This prophecy begins with a description of a future time, when "the mountain of the house of Yahweh" (v. 2) will be fully reestablished. It talks about a time when all people will seek the Lord (v. 3). It talks about a time when Jerusalem will be restored and a time of peace will be established (v. 4).

3. How does this relate to our Advent preparation?

Response: Isaiah's prophecy encourages his hearers to look forward to the time when the Lord will again reign in Jerusalem. It is also a warning to prepare for this time, which will come. In the context of Advent, it is an encouragement and exhortation to be ready for the time of the Lord's return.

MONDAY: Psalm 122 (Part 1)

A song of ascents. Of David.
I rejoiced in those who said to me,
"Let us go to the house of Yahweh."
Our feet are standing
within your gates, O Jerusalem—
Jerusalem that is built
as a city that is joined together,
where the tribes go up,
the tribes of Yah as a testimony for Israel,
to give thanks to the name of Yahweh.
For there the thrones sit for judgment,
thrones of David's house.
Pray for the peace of Jerusalem:
"May those who love you be at ease.

May peace be within your walls,
security within your palaces."
For the sake of my brothers and my friends,
I will say, "Peace be within you."
For the sake of the house of Yahweh our God,
I will seek your good.

Discussion Questions

1. This psalm is a "song of ascents." What is that?

   Response: Psalms 120–134 are called "song of ascents" in their titles. These psalms frequently mention "going up" or ascending to Jerusalem and traditionally played a role in the Feast of Tabernacles or Booths (Lev 23:33–44). The Feast of Booths was an observance that remembered the Israelites' time in the wilderness of Sinai. During this weeklong festival, the Israelites lived in tents to remember what God called them from and what God brought them to. It reminded them that God was faithful to his Word.

2. How does this relate to our Advent preparation?

   Response: We know that God is faithful. The Feast of Booths reminded the Israelites of this, that the God who was with them in the wilderness would bring them to the land he promised. The Lord has promised to return, and we know that he will be faithful to this promise. Since we know that he will return, we should prepare for his arrival.

TUESDAY: Psalm 122 (Part 2)

A song of ascents. Of David.
I rejoiced in those who said to me,
"Let us go to the house of Yahweh."
Our feet are standing
within your gates, O Jerusalem—
Jerusalem that is built
as a city that is joined together,
where the tribes go up,
the tribes of Yah as a testimony for Israel,
to give thanks to the name of Yahweh.
For there the thrones sit for judgment,
thrones of David's house.
Pray for the peace of Jerusalem:
"May those who love you be at ease.
May peace be within your walls,
security within your palaces."
For the sake of my brothers and my friends,
I will say, "Peace be within you."
For the sake of the house of Yahweh our God,
I will seek your good.

Discussion Questions

1. Where does the psalmist (the writer of the psalm—here, David) speak of going?

   Response: The psalmist and those with him are going to Jerusalem, where Yahweh lives. When their feet are in the gates of the city, they know they are in the presence of the Lord. This psalm was sung by pilgrim groups from the tribes of Israel (vv. 3–4) going to Jerusalem. When they arrived, they would be in God's presence.

2. What is prayed for in Psalm 122:5–9?

Response: The psalmist prays for the peace of Jerusalem. As the city of the presence of the Lord, it is necessary for Jerusalem to remain in peace. This peace is *shalom*, so it has to do with prosperity and success, not necessarily absence of war.

3. How does this relate to our Advent preparation?

Response: Jerusalem at peace (*shalom*) reminds us of the return of the Lord. As the pilgrims to Jerusalem prayed for the city to be at peace and cherished their arrival in its gates, so we should look forward to the return of our Lord, preparing our hearts for his return.

WEDNESDAY: Romans 13:11-14 (Part 1)

And do this because you know the time, that it is already the hour for you to wake up from sleep. For our salvation is nearer now than when we believed. The night is far gone, and the day has drawn near. Therefore let us throw off the deeds of darkness and put on the weapons of light. Let us live decently, as in the day, not in carousing and drunkenness, not in sexual immorality and licentiousness, not in strife and jealousy. But put on the Lord Jesus Christ and do not make provision for the desires of the flesh.

Discussion Questions

1. Verse 11 begins with "And do this..." What is being referred to?

   Response: Verses 8–10 discuss the necessity of loving one another and how all the commandments are summed up with "love your neighbor as yourself" (see also Lev 19:18; Mark 12:31–33; Gal 5:14; Jas 2:8). In verse 11, "do this" refers to loving your neighbor.

2. What is the reason to "do this" in verse 11?

   Response: The reason given is "because you know the time." This is clarified as "the hour for you to wake up from sleep." Here, waking from sleep is not about getting out of bed—it's about realizing that the return of the Lord is near. It's time to live with this in mind: "Our salvation is nearer now than when we believed."

3. How does this relate to our Advent preparation?

   Response: The Lord will return! The hour is near. One way to prepare for his return is to live as we have been commanded: to love our neighbors as ourselves.

THURSDAY: Romans 13:11-14 (Part 2)

And do this because you know the time, that it is already the hour for you to wake up from sleep. For our salvation is nearer now than when we believed. The night is far gone, and the day has drawn near. Therefore let us throw off the deeds of darkness and put on the weapons of light. Let us live decently, as in the day, not in carousing and drunkenness, not in sexual immorality and licentiousness, not in strife and jealousy. But put on the Lord Jesus Christ and do not make provision for the desires of the flesh.

Discussion Questions

1. What is the message of Romans 13:11?

   Response: Love others, because the time of the Lord's return is near.

2. What other things does Paul tell the Roman believers to do in verses 12–14?

   Response: Paul introduces the contrast of night and day, with night representing the period before Christ's return and daytime representing the return of Christ. He implies that it is still night—but that the night is almost over. Because of this, those who believe Christ will return should live as if it is daytime, even though it is still nighttime. Verse 13 gives specific examples:

- Live decently (cf. 1 Thess 4:12)
- No carousing (or excessive partying) or drunkenness
- No sexual immorality or licentiousness (lack of self restraint)
- No strife or jealousy

This is summed up with the commands to "put on" the Lord Jesus Christ (live decently, as if it is daytime) and to "not make provision for" the desires of the flesh (live in such a way as to leave the night).

3. How does this relate to our Advent preparation?

Response: Preparing for Advent means looking ahead to the return of Christ. It means to live in faith that he will return. It means leaving the "nighttime things" to the night, and even though it is still night, living as if it is daytime. It involves loving others because Christ loved us.

FRIDAY: Matthew 24:36-44 (Part 1)

But concerning that day and hour no one knows—not even the angels of heaven nor the Son—except the Father alone. For just as the days of Noah were, so the coming of the Son of Man will be. For as in the days before the flood they were eating and drinking, marrying and giving in marriage, until the day Noah entered into the ark. And they did not know anything until the deluge came and swept them all away. So also the coming of the Son of Man will be. Then there will be two men in the field; one will be taken and one left. Two women will be grinding at the mill; one will be taken and one left. Therefore be on the alert, because you do not know what day your Lord is coming! But understand this: that if the master of the house had known what watch of the night the thief was coming, he would have stayed awake and would not have let his house be broken into. For this reason you also must be ready, because the Son of Man is coming at an hour that you do not think he will come.

Discussion Questions

1. According to Matthew 24:36, who knows the time of the return of the Son of Man (the Messiah, Jesus)? And who doesn't know?

   Response: Only the Father knows the time. No one—not even angels in heaven or the Son—knows when the Son of Man will return.

2. Why is there a comparison with the days of Noah (vv. 37–39)?

Response: The comparison has to do with timing and expectation. In the days of Noah, even though the people knew of Noah's building of the ark, instead of living in anticipation of the flood, they chose to ridicule Noah, ignore the warning, and continue living in their sin. Everyone except Noah's family was destroyed when the flood came. It will be the same when the Son of Man returns: Those who do not believe he will return will be surprised and caught off guard when it happens.

3. How does this relate to our Advent preparation?

Response: If you prepare for something you believe will happen, you're ready when it actually does happen. Noah prepared for the flood. He built an ark. He was ready. The other people did not prepare; they were not ready—and they died. If we believe the Son of Man will return, we should prepare and be ready.

SATURDAY: Matthew 24:36-44 (Part 2)

> But concerning that day and hour no one knows—not even the angels of heaven nor the Son—except the Father alone. For just as the days of Noah were, so the coming of the Son of Man will be. For as in the days before the flood

they were eating and drinking, marrying and giving in marriage, until the day Noah entered into the ark. And they did not know anything until the deluge came and swept them all away. So also the coming of the Son of Man will be. Then there will be two men in the field; one will be taken and one left. Two women will be grinding at the mill; one will be taken and one left. Therefore be on the alert, because you do not know what day your Lord is coming! But understand this: that if the master of the house had known what watch of the night the thief was coming, he would have stayed awake and would not have let his house be broken into. For this reason you also must be ready, because the Son of Man is coming at an hour that you do not think he will come.

Discussion Questions

1. What did we learn about preparing for the Son of Man's return in the previous reading (Matt 24:36–39)?

   Response: Those who believe something will actually happen prepare for it, just like Noah believed God's warning about the flood and built the ark.

2. What other examples of being prepared are given (vv. 40–44)?

Response: Two men will be working in a field and one will be taken; two women will be working at the mill and one will be taken. In each example, one is prepared (the one taken), and one is not. The lesson, given in verse 42, is to be prepared "because you do not know what day your Lord is coming."

We also read the further example of being prepared for a thief: If the owner of the house knows a thief will break into his house, he will be prepared and protect it.

3. How does this relate to our Advent preparation?

Response: Preparation is important. If you believe something will happen, you prepare for it. If a hurricane is coming, you board up your house and evacuate the area. If we believe that Jesus, the Son of Man, is returning, then we should prepare for it.

WEEK TWO: Anticipation

Anticipation and preparation go together. If we do not anticipate that something will happen, chances are that we will not prepare for it either.

Anticipating Christ's return involves believing it will happen. It involves remembering what was foretold about him. As Christ was prophesied to come as a babe to Bethlehem (and to die upon the cross), so he is prophesied to come again to take us home.

Anticipating Christ's return prompts us to respond as John did: "Amen! Come, Lord Jesus!" (Rev 22:20).

SUNDAY: Isaiah 11:1-10 (Part 1)

> And a shoot will come out from the stump of Jesse,
>   and a branch from its roots will bear fruit.
> And the spirit of Yahweh shall rest on him—
>   a spirit of wisdom and understanding,
>   a spirit of counsel and might,
>   a spirit of knowledge and the fear of Yahweh.
>   And his breath is in the fear of Yahweh.
> And he shall judge not by his eyesight,
>   and he shall rebuke not by what he hears with
>   his ears.
> But he shall judge the poor with righteousness,
>   and he shall decide for the needy of the earth
>   with rectitude.

And he shall strike the earth with the rod of his mouth,

> and he shall kill the wicked person with the breath of his lips.

And righteousness shall be the belt around his waist,

> and faithfulness the belt around his loins.

And a wolf shall stay with a lamb,

> and a leopard shall lie down with a kid,

and a calf and a lion and a fatling together

> as a small boy leads them.

And a cow and a bear shall graze;

> their young shall lie down together.

> And a lion shall eat straw like the cattle.

And an infant shall play over a serpent's hole,

> and a toddler shall put his hand on a viper's hole.

They will not injure and they will not destroy on all of my holy mountain,

> for the earth will be full of the knowledge of Yahweh,

> as the waters cover the sea.

And this shall happen on that day:

the nations shall inquire of the root of Jesse,
which shall be standing as a signal to the peoples,
and his resting place shall be glorious.

Discussion Questions

1. Isaiah 11:1 speaks of someone named Jesse. Who is Jesse?

   Response: Jesse was King David's father (1 Sam 16:1–13). This verse introduces Jesse's family (the family, or "line," of King David) as the family that the Messiah would come from. It uses the picture of a stump (representing Jesse) with a new tree (representing the Messiah) growing from it.

2. What does Isaiah 11:2–5 tell us about this Messiah?

   Response: These verses tell us:

   - The spirit of Yahweh will rest on him (v. 2)
   - He will not judge by what he sees (v. 3)
   - He will not punish or decide disputes by what he hears (v. 3)
   - He will judge the poor with righteousness (v. 4)
   - He will advocate for the needy with fairness (v. 4)
   - He will judge the evil and the wicked (v. 4)
   - He will be righteous and faithful (v. 5)

3. How does this relate to our anticipation of Christ's return?

Response: Isaiah gives information about who the Messiah will be and what qualities he will have. The Messiah will be from the family line of Jesse, King David's father, and will judge with righteousness and fairness. This prophecy itself is an anticipation of the Messiah and looks to both his first coming, as a baby, and his second coming, as returning king.

MONDAY: Isaiah 11:1-10 (Part 2)

And a shoot will come out from the stump of Jesse,
    and a branch from its roots will bear fruit.
And the spirit of Yahweh shall rest on him—
        a spirit of wisdom and understanding,
        a spirit of counsel and might,
        a spirit of knowledge and the fear of Yahweh.
        And his breath is in the fear of Yahweh.
And he shall judge not by his eyesight,
        and he shall rebuke not by what he hears with
        his ears.
But he shall judge the poor with righteousness,
        and he shall decide for the needy of the earth
        with rectitude.
And he shall strike the earth with the rod of his
        mouth,

and he shall kill the wicked person with the
    breath of his lips.
And righteousness shall be the belt around his
waist,
    and faithfulness the belt around his loins.

And a wolf shall stay with a lamb,
    and a leopard shall lie down with a kid,
and a calf and a lion and a fatling together
    as a small boy leads them.
And a cow and a bear shall graze;
    their young shall lie down together.
    And a lion shall eat straw like the cattle.
And an infant shall play over a serpent's hole,
    and a toddler shall put his hand on a viper's
    hole.
They will not injure and they will not destroy on
all of my holy mountain,
    for the earth will be full of the knowledge of
    Yahweh,
    as the waters cover the sea.

And this shall happen on that day:

the nations shall inquire of the root of Jesse,
which shall be standing as a signal to the peoples,
and his resting place shall be glorious.

Discussion Questions

1. What did we learn about the Messiah from Isaiah 11:1-5?

   Response: Verse 1 indicated that the Messiah will come from King David's family line. Verses 2-5 listed many things—among them the idea that the Messiah will be a righteous judge of the poor and a fair advocate for the needy. See response two from Sunday's reading for more background.

2. Isaiah 11:6-9 describes animals and people, but they are put together in pairs that don't make much sense. What are the pairs mentioned? And what is the overall point of these verses?

   Response: The pairs mentioned are:

   - A wolf and a lamb (v. 6)
   - A leopard and a kid (baby goat) (v. 6)
   - A calf, a lion, and a "fatling" (young bull) as a group, with a young boy leading them (v. 6)
   - A cow and a bear, along with their offspring (v. 7)
   - A lion eating straw like a cow (v. 7)
   - An infant playing by a nest of snakes (v. 8)
   - A toddler playing by a nest of snakes (v. 8)

   These pairs would normally fear each other. Wolves attack lambs, leopards make meals of young goats, and lions and livestock don't coexist peacefully. Lions do not eat straw, and no right-minded parent would let their young children play by snakes. But these verses are talking about a future time, when the Messiah has come, and all of these relationships have been turned on their heads. It describes a time of unparalleled peace, not of enmity or mistrust or hatred.

3. How does this relate to our anticipation of Christ's return?

Response: We live in times marked by sin and its effects. It oozes into every part of our actions and thoughts and affects how we all interact with each other. When Christ returns, he will remove sin's hold on us, and God will look on us through the eyes of Christ. How incredible that will be! And how can we not look to that time with anticipation?

TUESDAY: Psalm 72:1-7, 18-19

> O God, give your judgments to the king,
> and your righteousness to the king's son.
> May he judge your people with righteousness,
> and your poor with justice.
> Let the mountains yield prosperity for the people,
> and the hills in righteousness.
> May he provide justice for the poor of the people,
> save the children of the needy,

and crush the oppressor.
May he live long while the sun endures
as long as the moon for all generations.
May he descend like rain on mown grass,
like showers watering the earth.
May what is right blossom in his days
and an abundance of peace, until the moon is no
more. ...

Blessed be Yahweh God, the God of Israel,
who alone does wonderful things.
And blessed be his glorious name forever,
and may the whole earth be filled with his glory.
Amen and Amen.

Discussion Questions

1. Psalm 72 is a psalm "of Solomon" and is seen as a prayer for the king (from our viewpoint, Christ). What is prayed for in this psalm?

Response: The following things are prayed for:

- The king will be wise and righteous (v. 1)
- The king will judge with righteousness and justice (v. 2)
- There will be prosperity and righteousness for the people (v. 3)
- Those who oppress the poor and needy will be crushed (v. 4)

- The king will have a long life (v. 5)
- The days of the king will be peaceful, prosperous, and righteous (vv. 6–7)

2. How does the psalm end (vv. 18–19)?

Response: The psalm ends with a benediction (a good word) proclaiming that it is God alone who does good things. This instructs that it is God alone who gives all good things, and the coming King is from God.

3. How does this relate to our anticipation of Christ's return?

Response: We look forward to when Christ will return and bring with him the times prophesied. As his children, we long for his reign and prepare for its arrival.

WEDNESDAY: Romans 15:4-13 (Part 1)

For whatever was written beforehand was written for our instruction, in order that through patient endurance and through the encouragement of the scriptures we may have hope. Now may the God of patient endurance and of encouragement grant you to be in agreement with one another, in accordance with Christ Jesus, so that with one mind you may glorify with one mouth the God and Father of our Lord Jesus Christ. Therefore

27

accept one another, just as Christ also has accepted you, to the glory of God.

For I say, Christ has become a servant of the circumcision on behalf of the truth of God, in order to confirm the promises to the fathers, and that the Gentiles may glorify God for his mercy, just as it is written,

> "Because of this, I will praise you among the Gentiles,
>> and I will sing praise to your name."

And again it says,

> "Rejoice, Gentiles, with his people."

And again,

> "Praise the Lord, all the Gentiles,
>> and let all the peoples praise him."

And again Isaiah says,

> "The root of Jesse will come,
>> even the one who rises to rule over the Gentiles;
> in him the Gentiles will put their hope."

Now may the God of hope fill you with all joy and peace in believing, so that you may abound in hope by the power of the Holy Spirit.

Discussion Questions

1. What does "whatever was written beforehand" (v. 4) refer to?

   Response: It refers to the writings of the prophets found in what we now call the Old Testament. Paul quotes some of these writings in verses 9–12. These Old Testament passages teach us about what is to come—the return of Christ. Through this, they give us hope.

2. Verses 5–6 include a benediction (recall yesterday's discussion on Psalm 72:18–19). What does the benediction say? And what does verse 7 direct the Roman Christians—who originally received this letter—to do?

   Response: The benediction encourages the Roman Christians to be in agreement with one another so that their unified testimony and actions will glorify God. In verses 1–4 Paul encouraged the Romans to focus on the needs of others, especially the weak (vv. 1–2), and to show the love of Christ to others (v. 3). When the Roman Christians do this—and when we do this—God is glorified. Verse 7 encourages Christians to "accept one another" by helping each other through weaknesses in the same way that Christ helped us by saving us.

3. How does this relate to our anticipation of Christ's return?

Response: In the same way that Christ helped us in our weakness through saving us, we can help others in their weaknesses. When we do this, we glorify God. Through our actions we testify that we believe the earlier writings of the prophets are true and that Christ will return. We anticipate his arrival through loving as he loved and serving as he served.

THURSDAY: Romans 15:4-13 (Part 2)

For whatever was written beforehand was written for our instruction, in order that through patient endurance and through the encouragement of the scriptures we may have hope. Now may the God of patient endurance and of encouragement grant you to be in agreement with one another, in accordance with Christ Jesus, so that with one mind you may glorify with one mouth the God and Father of our Lord Jesus Christ. Therefore accept one another, just as Christ also has accepted you, to the glory of God.

For I say, Christ has become a servant of the circumcision on behalf of the truth of God, in order to confirm the promises to the fathers, and that the Gentiles may glorify God for his mercy, just as it is written,

> "Because of this, I will praise you among
> the Gentiles,
>> and I will sing praise to your name."

And again it says,

> "Rejoice, Gentiles, with his people."

And again,

> "Praise the Lord, all the Gentiles,
>> and let all the peoples praise him."

And again Isaiah says,

> "The root of Jesse will come,
>> even the one who rises to rule over
>> the Gentiles;
> in him the Gentiles will put their hope."

Now may the God of hope fill you with all joy and peace in believing, so that you may abound in hope by the power of the Holy Spirit.

Discussion Questions

1. Romans 15:9–11 refers to several Old Testament Scriptures. What are those Scriptures, and what is the message?

   Response: The passages are Psalm 18:49; Deuteronomy 32:43; and Psalm 117:1. They recall how even the Old Testament testified that the Gentiles (non-Jewish people) would praise the Lord.

2. Romans 15:12 refers to Isaiah 11:10—the Scripture for Monday and Tuesday. What did we learn about Isaiah 11 on those days?

   Response: See the questions and responses from Monday and Tuesday. The overall message for believers today is that Christ addresses our deepest need, cleansing from sin. The one who does this is the one we hope in.

3. How does this relate to our anticipation of Christ's return?

   Response: Christ's sacrifice addressed our deepest need: cleansing from the sin that separates us from the Father. We anticipate his return by helping others with their needs: loving them in the same way that he loves us.

FRIDAY: Matthew 3:1-12 (Part 1)

Now in those days John the Baptist came preaching in the Judean wilderness and saying, "Repent, for the kingdom of heaven has come near!" For this is the one who was spoken about by the prophet Isaiah, saying,

> "The voice of one crying out in the wilderness,
> 'Prepare the way of the Lord,
>   make his paths straight.'"

Now John himself had his clothing made from camel's hair and a belt made of leather around his waist, and his food was locusts and wild honey. Then Jerusalem and all Judea and all the district around the Jordan were going out to him, and they were being baptized by him in the Jordan River as they confessed their sins.

But when he saw many of the Pharisees and Sadducees coming to his baptism, he said to them, "Offspring of vipers! Who warned you to flee from the coming wrath? Therefore produce fruit worthy of repentance! And do not think to say to yourselves, 'We have Abraham as father.' For I say to you that God is able to raise up children for Abraham from these stones! Already now the ax is positioned at the root of the trees; therefore every tree not producing good fruit is cut down and thrown into the fire. I baptize you with water for repentance, but the one who comes after me is more powerful than I am, whose sandals I am not worthy to carry. He will baptize you with the Holy Spirit and fire. His winnowing shovel is in his hand, and he will clean out his threshing floor and will gather his wheat into the storehouse, but he will burn up the chaff with unquenchable fire."

Discussion Questions

1. Who was John the Baptist?

   Response: John the Baptist was the son of Zechariah and Elizabeth (Luke 1:57-66). He was Jesus' cousin. And he was a prophet (Mark 1:1-8; Luke 3:1-20). His message was that the Messiah was coming: "Repent, for the kingdom of heaven has come near!" (Matt 3:2).

2. What did John look like and what did he eat (v. 4)? And where did he baptize (vv. 5-6)?

   Response: John had clothes made from camel's hair held up with a belt. He ate locusts (big grasshoppers) and honey. People from the surrounding area, comprised of Jerusalem and larger Judaea, came to the Jordan River to be baptized by John.

3. Why did John baptize?

Response: John baptized as a symbol. Baptism wasn't a new thing that John made up—it was a religious practice used to indicate purification. For John, baptism was tied to repentance and forgiveness. It indicated that one was preparing for the Messiah to come.

4. How does this relate to our anticipation of Christ's return?

Response: John the Baptist announced the coming of the kingdom. He baptized people to prepare them for its coming. His message to prepare for the kingdom through confession and repentance (vv. 2, 6) is also a message to us to do the same in anticipation of its arrival.

SATURDAY: Matthew 3:1-12 (Part 2)

Now in those days John the Baptist came preaching in the Judean wilderness and saying, "Repent, for the kingdom of heaven has come near!" For this is the one who was spoken about by the prophet Isaiah, saying,

"The voice of one crying out in the wilderness,
'Prepare the way of the Lord,
    make his paths straight.'"

Now John himself had his clothing made from camel's hair and a belt made of leather around his waist, and his food was locusts and wild honey. Then Jerusalem and all Judea and all the district around the Jordan were going out to him, and they were being baptized by him in the Jordan River as they confessed their sins.

But when he saw many of the Pharisees and Sadducees coming to his baptism, he said to them, "Offspring of vipers! Who warned you to flee from the coming wrath? Therefore produce fruit worthy of repentance! And do not think to say to yourselves, 'We have Abraham as father.' For I say to you that God is able to raise up children for Abraham from these stones! Already now the ax is positioned at the root of the trees; therefore every tree not producing good fruit is cut down and thrown into the fire. I baptize you with water for repentance, but the one who comes after me is more powerful than I am, whose sandals I am not worthy to carry. He will baptize you with the Holy Spirit and fire. His winnowing shovel is in his hand, and he will clean out his threshing floor and will gather his wheat into the storehouse, but he will burn up the chaff with unquenchable fire."

Discussion Questions

1. Who were the Pharisees and Sadducees?

    Response: Pharisees and Sadducees were the leading groups of Jews in the time of Jesus. The Pharisees required strict adherence to the (Old Testament) law. The Sadducees likely did as well, though they differed from the Pharisees on a few key points. The important thing to know about these groups is that they the religious leaders of the people and, more specifically, at the temple and synagogues.

2. What was John the Baptist's message to the Pharisees and Sadducees (vv. 7–12)?

    Response: John calls them "offspring of vipers" or, in some translations, a "brood of vipers." He equates them with snakes that sneakily slither and kill the unsuspecting. John warns them against trusting in their heritage as Jews (v. 9) and implies that they will be cut off from the promises of their Jewish heritage because they are not living and producing "good fruit" (v. 10). John notes that the baptism he offers is for repentance (which he implies they need) and that someone else— the Messiah—is coming (v. 11). Moreover, the Messiah will have no tolerance for them (v. 12).

3. How does this relate to our anticipation of Christ's return?

Response: Christ's return offers hope to those who prepare and anticipate but judgment to those who do not. John the Baptist's message is to be ready: The Messiah is coming, and he will not wait for you once he's here.

WEEK THREE: Joy

Preparation and anticipation have focused our thoughts and actions on the arrival of Christ. As this arrival draws closer, a natural consequence is joy. When the thing we have been waiting for gets closer and closer, joy increases.

When I was a boy, my dad was in the Navy. There were times he was away from home for months. We wrote letters—there was no email then—to keep in touch. If he was in port, he would call us. But as the day of his homecoming drew closer, our whole family grew excited. The joy started *before* he came home, when months turned to weeks, weeks turned to days, and days turned to hours.

Joy is a natural part of anticipating Christ's return as we consider what he has accomplished for us and what he will accomplish for us. Our Savior lives! Our King is returning! And he will take us home.

SUNDAY: Isaiah 35:1-10 (Part 1)

Wilderness and dry land shall be glad,
>and desert shall rejoice and blossom like the crocus.
It shall blossom abundantly,
>and it shall rejoice indeed with rejoicing and exulting.
The glory of Lebanon shall be given to it,

the majesty of Carmel and Sharon.
They are the ones who shall see the glory of
Yahweh,
    the majesty of our God.

Strengthen the weak hands
    and make the staggering knees firm.

Say to those who are hasty of heart,

"Be strong; you must not fear!
    Look! your God will come with vengeance,
with divine retribution.
    He is the one who will come and save you."

Then the eyes of the blind shall be opened,
    and the ears of the deaf shall be opened.
Then the lame shall leap like the deer,
    and the tongue of the dumb shall sing for joy,
for waters shall break forth in the wilderness
    and streams in the desert.
And the parched ground shall become a pool,
    and the thirsty ground springs of water.
Her resting place is in a settlement of jackals;
    the grass shall become like reeds and rushes.

And a highway shall be there, and a way,
    and it shall be called the way of holiness.
The unclean shall not travel through it,
    but it is for them, he who walks on the way;
    and fools shall not wander about.

No lion shall be there,
    and no ferocious wild beast shall go up it.
It shall not be found there,
    but the redeemed shall walk there.
And the ransomed of Yahweh shall return,
    and they shall come to Zion with rejoicing.
And everlasting joy shall be on their head;
    joy and gladness shall overtake them,
    and sorrow and sighing shall flee.

Discussion Questions

1. To understand the picture in Isaiah 35, we need to look at the chapter before for context. In Isaiah 34, the land and its inhabitants are under judgment. What is different with the picture in Isaiah 35:1–2?

   Response: The land rejoices and the desert is blooming (v. 1); the places that had been withering from drought are now where God's majesty will be seen (v. 2). God has returned to the land.

2. What sorts of descriptions are used in verse 3 and the first part of verse 4? How does this change at the end of verse 4?

   Response: Verses 3 and 4 describe someone with weak hands, staggering (feeble or shaking) knees, and a "hasty" heart (which perhaps indicates a quick-beating heart due to the situation). Overall, the description paints a picture of someone so afraid that they have physical symptoms of anxiety. But the last part of verse 4 encourages this very person to be strong, because the Lord will come. The person in the desolated setting of Isaiah 34, fearing what comes next, can rejoice and be strong because the Lord will come. And he brings vengeance with him.

3. How does this relate to joy during the Advent season?

Response: No matter what our present situation—even when we're living in desolation like that of Isaiah 34—we know that our God will save us. In the midst of tough times, we can rejoice: Our God will come!

MONDAY: Isaiah 35:1-10 (Part 2)

Wilderness and dry land shall be glad,
>and desert shall rejoice and blossom like the crocus.
It shall blossom abundantly,
>and it shall rejoice indeed with rejoicing and exulting.
The glory of Lebanon shall be given to it,
>the majesty of Carmel and Sharon.
They are the ones who shall see the glory of Yahweh,
>the majesty of our God.

Strengthen the weak hands
>and make the staggering knees firm.

Say to those who are hasty of heart,

"Be strong; you must not fear!
    Look! your God will come with vengeance,
with divine retribution.
    He is the one who will come and save you."

Then the eyes of the blind shall be opened,
    and the ears of the deaf shall be opened.
Then the lame shall leap like the deer,
    and the tongue of the dumb shall sing for joy,
for waters shall break forth in the wilderness
    and streams in the desert.
And the parched ground shall become a pool,
    and the thirsty ground springs of water.
Her resting place is in a settlement of jackals;
    the grass shall become like reeds and rushes.

And a highway shall be there, and a way,
    and it shall be called the way of holiness.
The unclean shall not travel through it,
    but it is for them, he who walks on the way;
    and fools shall not wander about.
No lion shall be there,
    and no ferocious wild beast shall go up it.
It shall not be found there,
    but the redeemed shall walk there.
And the ransomed of Yahweh shall return,
    and they shall come to Zion with rejoicing.
And everlasting joy shall be on their head;

> joy and gladness shall overtake them,
> and sorrow and sighing shall flee.

Discussion Questions

1. What are the opposites in Isaiah 35:5–7?

   Response: Opposites include:

   - The blind will see (v. 5)
   - The deaf will hear (v. 5)
   - The lame will walk (v. 6)
   - The speechless (dumb) will speak (v. 6)
   - Water will run through the desert (v. 6)
   - Dry (parched) ground will become a pool (v. 7)
   - A place filled with predators will become a place to rest (v. 7)

2. What place is described in Isaiah 35:8–10? Where is it?

   Response: This is the resting place from the end of verse 7—a place called Zion. The location Zion is a reference to Jerusalem and the time of the Lord's return.

3. How does this relate to joy during the Advent season?

   Response: The Lord will return and establish his people and his land—a cause for rejoicing when he does. But before then, even in the midst of unbearable circumstances, his people can look forward to his arrival and rejoice in the present because they know the future.

TUESDAY: Psalm 146:5-10

Blessed is the one whose help is the God of Jacob,
whose hope is on Yahweh as his God,
who made heaven and earth,
the sea and all that is in them,
the one who keeps faith forever,
who executes justice for the oppressed,
who gives food for the hungry.
Yahweh sets prisoners free;
Yahweh opens the eyes of the blind;
Yahweh raises up those bowed down;
Yahweh loves the righteous;
Yahweh protects the strangers.
He helps up the orphan and the widow,
but the way of the wicked he thwarts.

Yahweh will reign forever,
Your God, O Zion, throughout all generations.

Praise Yah.

Discussion Questions

1. According to Psalm 146:5, who is "blessed"?

Response: The first line of the verse notes that the one who relies on God is blessed. The second line of the verse—an example of a poetic technique called parallelism—indicates that the one who hopes upon Yahweh as God is blessed. These both point to the one who trusts in God for salvation as the one being blessed.

2. How is God described in Psalm 146:6–10?

Response: God (Yahweh) is described as:

- creating heaven and earth (v. 6)
- being faithful forever (v. 6)
- ensuring the oppressed see justice (v. 7)
- giving food to the hungry (v. 7)
- setting prisoners free (v. 7)
- restoring sight for the blind (v. 8)
- restoring those who are bent and broken (v. 8)
- loving the righteous (v. 8)
- protecting strangers (v. 9)
- helping orphans and widows (v. 9)
- thwarting the wicked (v. 9)
- reigning forever (v. 10)

3. How does this relate to joy during the Advent season?

Response: The faithful God who does the things described in verses 6-10 is our God. He is on the throne forever. He will return, and the thought of our King returning brings joy to our hearts.

WEDNESDAY: Luke 1:46-55

And Mary said,

"My soul exalts the Lord,
    and my spirit has rejoiced greatly in God my
    Savior,
because he has looked upon the humble state of
his female slave,
    for behold, from now on all generations will
    consider me blessed,
because the Mighty One has done great things for
me,
    and holy is his name.
And his mercy is for generation after generation
    to those who fear him.
He has done a mighty deed with his arm;
    he has dispersed the proud in the thoughts of
    their hearts.
He has brought down rulers from their thrones,
    and has exalted the lowly.

He has filled those who are hungry with good
things,
     and those who are rich he has sent away
     empty-handed.
He has helped Israel his servant,
     remembering his mercy,
just as he spoke to our fathers,
     to Abraham and to his descendants forever."

Discussion Questions

1. Why is Mary rejoicing?

   Response: Mary is rejoicing because despite her
   "humble state" (v. 48) she has been blessed by the Lord.
   The mercy of the Lord that she experienced is overwhelming and undeserved (v. 49–50), and she praises
   his name because of it.

2. How does this relate to joy during the Advent season?

   Response: The mercy we receive as a result of Jesus'
   first coming is similarly overwhelming and undeserved—and we rejoice because of it. We rejoice all the
   more at the thought of his second coming.

THURSDAY: James 5:7-10

Therefore be patient, brothers, until the coming of the Lord. Behold, the farmer waits for

the precious fruit of the soil, being patient concerning it until it receives the early and late rains. You also be patient. Strengthen your hearts, because the coming of the Lord is near. Brothers, do not complain against one another, in order that you may not be judged. Behold, the judge stands before the doors! Brothers, take as an example of perseverance and endurance the prophets who spoke in the name of the Lord.

Discussion Questions

1. Why are the readers and hearers of James told to be patient (Jas 5:7-8)?

   Response: They are told to be patient until "the coming of the Lord" (v. 7). The passage begins with "therefore" and is an exhortation to action built upon the previous verses (v. 1-6), which center on the judgment of the rich. James uses the example of a farmer (v. 7-8) who plants a crop and then waits for harvest time. In the same way, James is telling his hearers that in the midst of everything unjust going on around them, they need to be patient and wait because the Lord is coming back. He will reap the harvest of his field.

2. James indicates that instruction follows when he uses the term "brothers." It is James' way of getting the attention of his hearers and readers. Where does he

use "brothers" in this passage, and what instruction is he giving?

Response: In this passage, James uses "brothers" (which could also be read as "brothers and sisters") three times:

- Verse 7, with instruction about patience (see question 1 above)
- Verse 9, with instruction about not complaining against each other
- Verse 10, with instruction to remember the prophets as examples of perseverance and endurance

In each of these instructions James is telling his readers and hearers to be patient and gracious in relationships, because they know the Lord will return and set everything right.

3. How does this relate to joy during the Advent season?

Response: We know the Lord will come, and we patiently—and sometimes not so patiently—await his arrival. Knowing he will come and set the wrong things right can give us joy while we wait.

FRIDAY: Matthew 11:2-11 (Part 1)

Now when John heard in prison the deeds of Christ, he sent word by his disciples and said to him, "Are you the one who is to come, or should we look for another?" And Jesus answered and said to them, "Go and tell John what you hear and see: the blind receive sight and the lame walk, lepers are cleansed and the deaf hear, and the dead are raised, and the poor have good news announced to them. And whoever is not offended by me is blessed."

Now as these were going away, Jesus began to speak to the crowds concerning John: "What did you go out into the wilderness to see? A reed shaken by the wind? But what did you go out to see? A man dressed in soft clothing? Behold, those who wear soft clothing are in the houses of kings. But why did you go out? To see a prophet? Yes, I tell you, and even more than a prophet! It is this man about whom it is written:

> 'Behold, I am sending my messenger before your face,
>> who will prepare your way before you.'

Truly I say to you, among those born of women there has not arisen one greater than John the Baptist. But the one who is least in the kingdom of heaven is greater than he."

Discussion Questions

1. What did John the Baptist's disciples ask Jesus (vv. 2–3)?

   Response: John the Baptist was in prison, but he heard about what Jesus had been doing. John's question was, basically, "Are you the Messiah?" The purpose of John the Baptist's preaching was to announce the Messiah's arrival (see Friday and Saturday readings from Week 2). John, who had earlier baptized Jesus, probably asked the question for the benefit of his disciples.

2. How did Jesus respond (vv. 4–6)?

   Response: Jesus didn't explicitly confirm or deny that he was the Messiah. Instead, he pointed to the things he did (vv. 4–5) as evidence of who he was. The blind see, the deaf hear, the lame walk, lepers are cleansed, and the dead have been raised. These are all things that people expected the Messiah to do.

3. How does this relate to joy during the Advent season?

   Response: The Messiah was with John the Baptist's disciples if they stopped to look and notice him. Jesus was doing the things that the Messiah was expected to do—and John the Baptist's disciples would have known this. Can you imagine their joy as they returned to John?

SATURDAY: Matthew 11:2-11 (Part 2)

Now when John heard in prison the deeds of
Christ, he sent word by his disciples and said
to him, "Are you the one who is to come, or
should we look for another?" And Jesus answered and said to them, "Go and tell John
what you hear and see: the blind receive sight
and the lame walk, lepers are cleansed and
the deaf hear, and the dead are raised, and
the poor have good news announced to them.
And whoever is not offended by me is blessed."

Now as these were going away, Jesus began to speak to the crowds concerning John:
"What did you go out into the wilderness to
see? A reed shaken by the wind? But what did
you go out to see? A man dressed in soft clothing? Behold, those who wear soft clothing are
in the houses of kings. But why did you go out?
To see a prophet? Yes, I tell you, and even more
than a prophet! It is this man about whom it is
written:

> 'Behold, I am sending my messenger
> before your face,
>   who will prepare your way before
> you.'

Truly I say to you, among those born of wom-
en there has not arisen one greater than John

the Baptist. But the one who is least in the kingdom of heaven is greater than he."

Discussion Questions

1. What did Jesus say to the crowd after John the Baptist's disciples left (vv. 7–11)?

Response: Crowds followed John, but less because of his message and more because of his peculiarity. In this reading, Jesus challenges the crowd regarding John the Baptist—a judgment on the crowd, not John. Jesus essentially says: You don't go into the wilderness to see the wind blow, or to see people in regal clothes. But one might go to the wilderness to see a prophet.

In Israel's history, prophets seem to be out in the wilderness much of the time. And in John's case, this is true. But Jesus says it is more than that, because John is more than a prophet. John is the messenger (compare Mal 3:1) who prepared the way for the Messiah.

2. How does this relate to joy during the Advent season?

Response: The Old Testament prophets indicated that there would be a messenger announcing the arrival of the Messiah. This happened as John the Baptist announced the coming of Jesus. We have been told that Jesus will come again, and that there are signs of his coming. This should cause joy in our hearts! Our Messiah will return, and he will make us aware of his coming.

WEEK FOUR: Incarnation

Incarnation is a mysterious thing that we cannot fully comprehend: How the Son of the living God took on flesh to be like us, to save us. Though we do not understand how it happened, we can, like the author of Hebrews, appreciate it greatly:

> Therefore, since the children share in blood and flesh, he also in like manner shared in these same things, in order that through death he could destroy the one who has the power of death, that is, the devil, and could set free these who through fear of death were subject to slavery throughout all their lives. For surely he is not concerned with angels, but he is concerned with the descendants of Abraham. Therefore he was obligated to be made like his brothers in all respects, in order that he could become a merciful and faithful high priest in the things relating to God, in order to make atonement for the sins of the people. For in that which he himself suffered when he was tempted, he is able to help those who are tempted (Hebrews 2:14–18).

SUNDAY: Isaiah 7:10-16

And Yahweh continued to speak to Ahaz, saying, "Ask for a sign for yourself from Yahweh
God; make it deep as Sheol or make it high as
above." But Ahaz said, "I will not ask, and I
will not put Yahweh to the test."

Then he said, "Hear, house of David! Is it
too little for you to make men weary, that you
should also make my God weary? Therefore
the Lord himself will give you a sign. Look!
the virgin is with child and she is about to give
birth to a son, and she shall call his name 'God
with us.' He shall eat curds and honey until he
knows to reject the evil and to choose the good.
For before the boy knows to reject the evil and
to choose the good, the land whose two kings
you dread will be abandoned.

Discussion Questions

1. Who is Ahaz? And what is the larger context of
this passage?

   Response: Ahaz is the king of Judah (Isa 7:1). The context involves a coalition of kings who want a different king in Judah (the "son of Tabeel" or "ben Tabeel,"
   Isa 7:6). In Isaiah 7:3, Yahweh sends Isaiah the prophet
   to Ahaz with a message that Judah will prevail, and
   Ahaz will remain king (Isa 7:4, 7).

2. What does Yahweh tell Ahaz to do (vv. 10–11) and what is Ahaz' response (v. 12)?

Response: Yahweh tells Ahaz to ask for a sign—any sign—to verify that what Isaiah says is true. It could be as big and audacious as Ahaz wants ("make it as deep as Sheol or make it high as above," v. 11).

Ahaz' response is refusal. Why does Ahaz refuse? It may be because when the sign happens, he will be responsible to act—that is, once the sign occurs, the next thing will happen.

3. What sign does Yahweh give?

Response: Despite Ahaz' refusal, Yahweh provides a sign: a virgin (or young woman or maiden) is pregnant and about to give birth. Before her child is old enough to know good from evil, the coalition of kings who are rising against Judah will be destroyed, and Judah will be preserved. The child's name is "God with us," or "Immanuel"; this is significant, because the name shows that the presence of the Lord will be with Judah.

4. How does this passage show that the incarnation is important to remember during Advent?

Response: This same passage, foretelling the birth of a son named Immanuel, is cited in Matthew 1:18–25 (see Friday and Saturday's upcoming reading). In Matthew 1:22, the prophecy of Isaiah 7:14 is described as fulfilled by Jesus' birth. The ultimate fulfillment of Ahaz' refused sign is the birth of the Messiah—the arrival of Jesus, who is God in the flesh.

MONDAY: Psalm 80:1-7; 17-19 (Part 1)

Give ear, O shepherd of Israel,
who leads Joseph like a flock.
Shine forth, you who sits enthroned above the cherubim.
Before Ephraim, Benjamin, and Manasseh,
stir up your power
and come for our salvation.
O God, restore us,
and cause your face to shine that we may be saved.
O Yahweh God of hosts,
how long will you be angry
against the prayer of your people?
You have fed them the bread of tears;
you have given them tears to drink in full measure.
You have made us an object of strife to our neighbors,
and our enemies mock among themselves.
O God of hosts, restore us
and cause your face to shine that we may be saved. ...

Let your hand be on the man of your right hand,
on the son of humankind whom you made strong for yourself.

Then we will not turn back from you.
Restore us to life, and we will proclaim your name.
O Yahweh God of hosts, restore us;
cause your face to shine that we may be saved.

Discussion Questions

1. What does the psalmist (here, Asaph) ask of God (vv. 2–3, 7)?

   Response: Israel is out of favor with God and needs to be restored and put back into favor. Asaph pleas for restoration.

2. Why do the people need restoration (vv. 4–6)?

   Response: The people need restoration because they have acted against God. In this psalm, the people have prayed, and their prayers have not been answered; God has not acted in response to their request. They desire to be restored so that their prayers will be heard.

3. How does this passage show that the incarnation is important to remember during Advent?

   Response: The incarnation is the restoration of God's people into right relationship with him. Without the incarnate Messiah, we can't approach God. Instead, we stand apart from him. With the incarnate Messiah, though, we can approach God. We have the restoration that Asaph desires.

TUESDAY: Psalm 80:1-7; 17-19 (Part 2)

Give ear, O shepherd of Israel,
who leads Joseph like a flock.
Shine forth, you who sits enthroned above the
cherubim.
Before Ephraim, Benjamin, and Manasseh,
stir up your power
and come for our salvation.
O God, restore us,
and cause your face to shine that we may be saved.
O Yahweh God of hosts,
how long will you be angry
against the prayer of your people?
You have fed them the bread of tears;
you have given them tears to drink in full measure.
You have made us an object of strife to our
neighbors,
and our enemies mock among themselves.
O God of hosts, restore us
and cause your face to shine that we may be
saved. ...

Let your hand be on the man of your right hand,
on the son of humankind whom you made strong
for yourself.
Then we will not turn back from you.
Restore us to life, and we will proclaim your name.
O Yahweh God of hosts, restore us;
cause your face to shine that we may be saved.

Discussion Questions

1. Who does "the man of your right hand" (v. 17) refer to?

   Response: In the original context of the psalm, it referred to the king of Israel. But since the king of Israel is God's anointed one, it ultimately refers to Christ.

2. What does "restore us to life, and we will proclaim your name" (v. 18) mean? Are the Israelites bargaining with God?

   Response: Remember that Israel is a nation in a covenant relationship with God (Exod 6:7; Lev 26:12; Jer 30:22). The people have moved away from God but need to return. God, however, has not moved. The people are not bargaining; they need to be brought back to God and *then* they can rightly proclaim God's name.

3. How does this passage show that the incarnation is important to remember during Advent?

   Response: The passage points to Christ as the ultimate representative of God on earth, as king of God's people. It is this king who will restore the people to God.

WEDNESDAY: Romans 1:1-7 (Part 1)

> Paul, a slave of Christ Jesus, called to be an apostle, set apart for the gospel of God, which he promised previously through his prophets

in the holy scriptures, concerning his Son, who was born a descendant of David according to the flesh, who was declared Son of God in power according to the Holy Spirit by the resurrection from the dead of Jesus Christ our Lord, through whom we have received grace and apostleship for the obedience of faith among all the Gentiles on behalf of his name, among whom you also are the called of Jesus Christ. To all those in Rome who are loved by God, called to be saints. Grace to you and peace from God our Father and the Lord Jesus Christ.

Discussion Questions

1. The book of Romans is actually a letter from Paul to the people of the church in Rome. How is this reflected in the start of letter?

Response: Ancient letters began with three basic parts: Declaration of sender, declaration of recipient, and some sort of greeting statement. In letters between people, these were very brief: "Bruce, to Alfred: Greetings." The beginnings of Paul's letters found in the New Testament, however, are longer. Romans is the longest—Paul used the letter's start as an opportunity to assert his own authority as an apostle. In Romans, he appears to spend six verses (vv. 1–6) introducing himself. In reality, five of those verses (vv. 2–6) are focused on the gospel.

2. What does Paul say about Jesus (vv. 3–6)?

Response: Paul tells the Romans:

- The gospel concerns the Son of God (v. 3)
- The Son of God was a descendant of David ("according to the flesh," which points to his incarnation; v. 3)
- The sonship of the Son of God was proven through the resurrection (v. 4)
- Grace and apostleship came to the Gentiles (or "nations," here meaning non-Jewish people) through Jesus (v. 5)
- The Romans are among those who are called by Jesus (v. 6)

3. How does this passage show that the incarnation is important to remember during Advent?

Response: Jesus, the Son of God, was human (v. 3), but he overcame death (v. 4) and brought salvation to the nations (vv. 5–6). God became the perfect man and did what no sinful man could do: He called us together as his own and stands before God as our advocate. This is an awesome, precious thing.

THURSDAY: Romans 1:1-7 (Part 2)

> Paul, a slave of Christ Jesus, called to be an apostle, set apart for the gospel of God, which

he promised previously through his prophets in the holy scriptures, concerning his Son, who was born a descendant of David according to the flesh, who was declared Son of God in power according to the Holy Spirit by the resurrection from the dead of Jesus Christ our Lord, through whom we have received grace and apostleship for the obedience of faith among all the Gentiles on behalf of his name, among whom you also are the called of Jesus Christ. To all those in Rome who are loved by God, called to be saints. Grace to you and peace from God our Father and the Lord Jesus Christ.

Discussion Questions

1. What did Paul say about Jesus' incarnation (v. 3)?

   Response: Paul says that the Son of God was a descendant of David. This means that the Son of God was a member of David's family—so, "of the stump of Jesse," David's father, as we learned from Isaiah 11:1 (Sunday of Week 2). Paul also says that this was "according to the flesh," a statement about the human nature of Christ.

2. Why is this important to Paul at the beginning of his Letter to the Romans?

   Response: In the start of the letter, Paul positions himself as apostle of Christ, proclaiming the gospel of

God. He defines the gospel something promised by the prophets in the Scriptures (v. 2) that is about the Son (v. 3). In verses 3–5, Paul shows how Jesus fits the role described for the promised Son. He shows how Jesus is the gospel, with Jesus as a human member of David's family but also as a Son of God who conquered death. These are the main components of the gospel Paul preaches to the Romans.

3. How does this passage show that the incarnation is important to remember during Advent?

Response: The passage reminds us that Jesus is human and divine. It reminds us that our Mediator and Advocate before God knows us because he is like us.

FRIDAY: Matthew 1:18-25 (Part 1)

Now the birth of Jesus Christ occurred in this way. His mother Mary had been betrothed to Joseph, but before they came together, she was found to be pregnant by the Holy Spirit. So Joseph her husband, being righteous and not wanting to disgrace her, intended to divorce her secretly. But as he was considering these things, behold, an angel of the Lord appeared to him in a dream, saying, "Joseph, son of David, do not be afraid to take Mary as your wife, for what has been conceived in her is from the Holy Spirit. And she will give birth to a son, and you will call his name 'Jesus,' because he will save his people from their sins." Now all this happened in order that what was spoken by the Lord through the prophet would be fulfilled, saying,

> "Behold, the virgin will become pregnant and will give birth to a son,
>   and they will call his name Emmanuel,"

which is translated, "God with us." And Joseph, when he woke up from sleep, did as the angel of the Lord commanded him, and he took his wife and did not have sexual relations with her until she gave birth to a son. And he called his name Jesus.

Discussion Questions

1. What do we learn about Joseph from this passage (vv. 18–21)?

Response: We learn the following:

- Joseph and Mary were engaged to be married (v. 18)
- Mary was pregnant, and Joseph was not the father (v. 18)
- Joseph wanted to get divorced (v. 19)

- An angel appeared to Joseph and convinced him to stay with Mary (vv. 20-21)
- Joseph married Mary and raised Jesus as his own son (vv. 24-25)

2. What did the angel say to convince Joseph (vv. 20-21)?

Response: The angel did not contradict Joseph. Mary was indeed pregnant, and Joseph indeed was not the father. Instead, the angel offered an alternate solution: The Holy Spirit was responsible (v. 20). And the angel gave new information: The child was a boy; he would be named "Jesus"; and he would save people from their sins (v. 21).

3. How does this passage show that the incarnation is important to remember during Advent?

Response: As a result of the incarnation, Jesus—fully God and fully man—saves us from our sin.

SATURDAY: Matthew 1:18-25 (Part 2)

Now the birth of Jesus Christ occurred in this way. His mother Mary had been betrothed to Joseph, but before they came together, she was found to be pregnant by the Holy Spirit. So Joseph her husband, being righteous and not wanting to disgrace her, intended to divorce her secretly. But as he was considering these things, behold, an angel of the Lord appeared to him in a dream, saying, "Joseph, son of David, do not be afraid to take Mary as your wife, for what has been conceived in her is from the Holy Spirit. And she will give birth to a son, and you will call his name 'Jesus,' because he will save his people from their sins." Now all this happened in order that what was spoken by the Lord through the prophet would be fulfilled, saying,

> "Behold, the virgin will become pregnant and will give birth to a son,
>   and they will call his name
> Emmanuel,"

which is translated, "God with us." And Joseph, when he woke up from sleep, did as the angel of the Lord commanded him, and he took his wife and did not have sexual relations with her until she gave birth to a son. And he called his name Jesus.

Discussion Questions

1. Verses 22–23 gives a reason why "all this happened." What is that reason?

Response: The reason is so that the word of the Lord would be fulfilled. Matthew ties this with Isaiah 7:14 (see Sunday's questions on Isaiah 7:10-16), which speaks of a young woman, or virgin, giving birth to a son. Matthew sees Jesus' birth as the ultimate fulfillment of that prophecy.

2. How can this passage be a fulfillment of the prophecy if Jesus wasn't named "Emmanuel"?

Response: The name Jesus comes from the Greek form of the name Joshua. Joshua, the leader of the Israelites after Moses, led the Israelites from the wilderness into the promised land. The name Joshua means "Yahweh is salvation." Emmanuel (or Immanuel) means "God with us." These are not the same words, but we understand Jesus' birth as the fulfillment of Isaiah 7:14 because Matthew tells us that this Jesus, born to Mary and Joseph, is the is the fulfillment of the prophecy—Jesus is Emmanuel.

3. How does this passage show that the incarnation is important to remember during Advent?

Response: This passage reminds us that Jesus is both human and divine. It reminds us that God became human and that he will, as the angel in Matthew puts it, "save his people from their sins." This salvation, possible through the incarnation, is precious.

YEAR B
ADVENT READINGS

Year B of the three-year liturgical cycle focuses on Mark for its gospel readings. Because Mark is the shortest of the Synoptic Gospels, the Gospel of John is also used. The coming of the Son of Man and the abomination of desolation, from Mark 13, call us to prepare for the second advent. The beginning of Mark's Gospel (Mark 1) quotes Isaiah 40 to open our eyes to Jesus before recalling the ministry of John the Baptist to anticipate Jesus' arrival. Selections from John 1—including another quotation of Isaiah 40—draw us to the joy of being in the light announced by John the Baptist. And Luke's account of Jesus' birth (Luke 1) tells us of the wonder of the incarnation.

WEEK ONE: Preparation

In this first week of Advent, our goal is to set our minds on what is coming. Remembering and considering prophecies about Christ's second coming is about preparing our minds and our thinking—about setting our minds on what is above. But preparation also involves action. If we are preparing for a hurricane, we don't only watch weather reports to verify that we are in its path—we also prepare the house, store supplies, and create an evacuation plan.

Preparation for the coming of Christ means remembering what we have been told about his coming and actively preparing for his arrival.

SUNDAY: Isaiah 64:1-9

Would that you would tear the heavens and come down;
    the mountains would quake before you,
as fire kindles brushwood,
    the fire causes water to boil,
to make your name known to your adversaries,
    that the nations might tremble from your
    presence.

When you did terrible deeds which we did not
expect, you came down;

the mountains quaked because of your
presence.

And since ancient times they have not heard,
    have not listened,
no eye has seen a God except you;
    he acts for the one who waits for him.

You meet with the one who rejoices,
    one who does righteousness.
In your ways they remember you.
    Look! You were angry and we sinned against
    them in ancient times and we were saved.
And we all have become like the unclean,
    and all our deeds of justice like a menstrual
    cloth,
And we all wither like a leaf,
    and our iniquities take us away like the wind.
And there is no one who calls on your name,
    who pulls himself up to keep hold of you,
for you have hidden your face from us,
    and melted us into the hand of our iniquity.
Yet now Yahweh, you are our father;
    we are the clay and you are our potter,
    and we all are the work of your hand.

You must not be exceedingly angry, Yahweh,
    and you must not remember iniquity forever!

Look! Behold, now! We all are your people!

Discussion Questions

1. Who is the subject of this passage? Who is the one referred to as "you"?

   Response: The "you" of the passage is God, Yahweh—as seen in vv. 8-9.

2. What is the subject of the passage asked to do (vv. 1-2)?

   Response: The subject, Yahweh, is asked to "tear the heavens" and come down to reveal himself as well as to make his name known among those who oppose him. He is asked to come and to protect and restore those who are his.

3. Why is he asked to put aside his anger, and to not remember iniquity (v. 9)?

   Response: Yahweh's people have sinned (vv. 5-7), but they now recognize their place before him (v. 8) and ask him to put aside his just anger and come to restore them.

4. How does this relate to our Advent preparation?

   Response: Looking ahead to the advent of the Lord involves remembering why he needed to come. In this passage, Israel remembers its sin, knows it deserves wrath, and yet asks Yahweh to return anyway. Advent preparation begins with remembering how sin has corrupted us and relying upon God to rescue us from it.

MONDAY: Psalm 80:1-7, 17-19 (Part 1)

Give ear, O shepherd of Israel,
who leads Joseph like a flock.
Shine forth, you who sits enthroned above the
cherubim.
Before Ephraim, Benjamin, and Manasseh,
stir up your power
and come for our salvation.
O God, restore us,
and cause your face to shine that we may be saved.
O Yahweh God of hosts,
how long will you be angry
against the prayer of your people?
You have fed them the bread of tears;
you have given them tears to drink in full measure.
You have made us an object of strife to our
neighbors,
and our enemies mock among themselves.
O God of hosts, restore us
and cause your face to shine that we may be
saved. ...

Let your hand be on the man of your right hand,
on the son of humankind whom you made strong
for yourself.
Then we will not turn back from you.
Restore us to life, and we will proclaim your name.
O Yahweh God of hosts, restore us;
cause your face to shine that we may be saved.

Discussion Questions

1. This psalm includes petition (making a request). What is the request (vv. 3, 7, 17)?

   Response: The request is for restoration and salvation.

2. Why does the request need to be made? What needs to be restored?

   Response: God's people had wandered away, and they needed to be restored to proper relationship. God was rightly angry with his people (v. 4). Their enemies no longer feared them because their God was not with them. They were apart from God and needed to be saved and restored to power.

3. How does this relate to our Advent preparation?

   Response: Only God can restore his people, but to be restored, his people need the Messiah to bring them back. This is Advent; God's people are preparing for his return by making themselves ready and asking for him to come back to them.

TUESDAY: Psalm 80:1-7, 17-19 (Part 2)

> Give ear, O shepherd of Israel,
> who leads Joseph like a flock.
> Shine forth, you who sits enthroned above the cherubim.

Before Ephraim, Benjamin, and Manasseh,
stir up your power
and come for our salvation.
O God, restore us,
and cause your face to shine that we may be saved.
O Yahweh God of hosts,
how long will you be angry
against the prayer of your people?
You have fed them the bread of tears;
you have given them tears to drink in full measure.
You have made us an object of strife to our
neighbors,
and our enemies mock among themselves.
O God of hosts, restore us
and cause your face to shine that we may be
saved. ...

Let your hand be on the man of your right hand,
on the son of humankind whom you made strong
for yourself.
Then we will not turn back from you.
Restore us to life, and we will proclaim your name.
O Yahweh God of hosts, restore us;
cause your face to shine that we may be saved.

Discussion Questions

1. Who is making the request?

   Response: The people of Israel, here represented as Joseph (v. 1), are the ones making the request. Joseph's younger brother Benjamin as well as his sons Ephraim and Manasseh (v. 2) are also mentioned in connection with Joseph.

2. Who is being asked?

   Response: The one being asked is the "shepherd of Israel" (v. 1), more directly called God (v. 3) and "Yahweh God of hosts" (vv. 4, 19).

3. How does this relate to our Advent preparation?

   Response: Advent is a term that represents the coming of the Messiah. In Psalm 80, the need for restoration and salvation is recognized and requested. God himself is petitioned to return and restore his people, who promise to remember him and proclaim his name (v. 18). The one they are requesting is the Messiah. They are preparing for him to come.

WEDNESDAY: 1 Corinthians 1:3-9 (Part 1)

> Grace to you and peace from God our Father and the Lord Jesus Christ.

I give thanks to my God always concerning you, because of the grace of God which was given to you in Christ Jesus, that in everything you were made rich in him, in all speech and all knowledge, just as the testimony about Christ has been confirmed in you, so that you do not lack in any spiritual gift as you eagerly await the revelation of our Lord Jesus Christ, who will also confirm you until the end, blameless in the day of our Lord Jesus Christ. God is faithful, by whom you were called to fellowship with his Son Jesus Christ our Lord.

Discussion Questions

1. This section of text (1:4-9) is called a "thanksgiving." What is Paul giving thanks for?

   Response: Paul is giving thanks:

   - that the Corinthians received the grace of God when they received Jesus Christ (v. 4)
   - that they were "made rich in him" in everything they said and learned (v. 5)
   - that their testimony about Christ was confirmed in them (v. 6, 8)
   - that they lack nothing in spiritual gifts (v. 7)
   - that they eagerly await the "revelation" (return, revealing) of Jesus Christ (v. 7)

2. Why is Paul thankful that the Corinthians were "made rich in him" (1:5)?

Response: For Paul, being made "rich" in Christ does not involve wealth or money. Instead, it is about understanding the grace of God, which is received through Christ Jesus. This made the Corinthians rich—as it also does us today—in that the most basic need of our lives, forgiveness of sin, is fully met. This is God's grace. It should permeate our being and be reflected in what we say and do.

3. How does this relate to our Advent preparation?

Response: We prepare for Advent by remembering the grace of God in our lives and by sharing the message of that grace with others.

THURSDAY: 1 Corinthians 1:3-9 (Part 2)

Grace to you and peace from God our Father and the Lord Jesus Christ.

I give thanks to my God always concerning you, because of the grace of God which was given to you in Christ Jesus, that in everything you were made rich in him, in all speech and all knowledge, just as the testimony about Christ has been confirmed in you, so that you do not lack in any spiritual gift as you eagerly await the revelation of our Lord Jesus Christ, who will also confirm you until the end, blameless in the day of our Lord Jesus Christ. God is faithful, by whom you were called to fellowship with his Son Jesus Christ our Lord.

Discussion Questions

1. Review the first question and response to yesterday's reading by remembering the things for which Paul gave thanks. In which things do you give thanks to God?

   Response: Talk with your family.

2. What does it mean that the Corinthians' testimony about Christ was confirmed?

   Response: "Testimony" is what you say or do. When you are in a courtroom on the witness stand, you give testimony by remembering what happened and giving those in the room an accurate account. Testimony is confirmed when someone else gives a similar account of the same event. Paul gives thanks that what the Corinthians testify about Christ is true and that their testimony has been confirmed by how they live their lives.

3. How does this relate to our Advent preparation?

   Response: The Corinthians "eagerly awaited" the return of Jesus (v. 8). One way they did this was by ensuring their testimony—what they said about Jesus—was true. We can prepare for Jesus' return by remembering the things he did and telling them to others.

FRIDAY: Mark 13:24-37 (Part 1)

The Arrival of the Son of Man

"But in those days, after that tribulation,

> 'the sun will be darkened
>> and the moon will not give its light,
> and the stars will be falling from heaven,
>> and the powers in the heavens will
> be shaken.'

And then they will see the Son of Man arriving in the clouds with great power and glory. And then he will send out the angels, and will gather the elect together from the four winds, from the end of the earth to the end of heaven.

The Parable of the Fig Tree

"Now learn the parable from the fig tree: Whenever its branch has already become tender and puts forth its leaves, you know that summer is near. So also you, when you see these things happening, know that he is near, at the door. Truly I say to you that this generation will never pass away until all these things take place! Heaven and earth will pass away, but my words will never pass away.

The Unknown Day and Hour

"But concerning that day or hour no one knows—not even the angels in heaven nor the Son—except the Father. Watch out! Be alert, because you do not know when the time is! It is like a man away on a journey, who left his house and gave his slaves authority—to each one his work—and to the doorkeeper he gave orders that he should be on the alert. Therefore be on the alert, for you do not know when the master of the house is coming—whether in the evening, or at midnight, or when the rooster crows, or early in the morning—lest he arrive suddenly and find you sleeping. And what I say to you, I say to everyone: Be on the alert!"

Discussion Questions

1. What is "tribulation" (Mark 13:24)?

Response: Previous verses (vv. 14–23) recall the "abomination of desolation," which was mentioned by Daniel (Dan 9:27; 11:31). The abomination of desolation is a reference to an actual event, the desecration of the temple in Jerusalem by Antiochus IV Epiphanes in 168 BC. Here, Jesus mentions an actual historical event as a signal to his listeners: If they should hear of another desecration, it is a signal that trouble is upon them. This time of trouble is known as the tribulation.

2. What happens after the tribulation (Mark 13:24-27)?

Response: After the tribulation, heavenly signs will appear, "the powers in heaven will be shaken" (vv. 24-25), and the Son of Man, Jesus, will come.

3. How does this relate to our Advent preparation?

Response: We can prepare for the return of Jesus by being aware of the signs of his coming. Our Advent preparation involves remembering these things that Jesus told us about his return and telling them to others so we may all be focused on his arrival.

SATURDAY: Mark 13:24-37 (Part 2)

The Arrival of the Son of Man

"But in those days, after that tribulation,

'the sun will be darkened
and the moon will not give its light,
and the stars will be falling from heaven,
and the powers in the heavens will
be shaken.'

And then they will see the Son of Man arriving in the clouds with great power and glory.

And then he will send out the angels, and will gather the elect together from the four winds, from the end of the earth to the end of heaven.

The Parable of the Fig Tree

"Now learn the parable from the fig tree: Whenever its branch has already become tender and puts forth its leaves, you know that summer is near. So also you, when you see these things happening, know that he is near, at the door. Truly I say to you that this generation will never pass away until all these things take place! Heaven and earth will pass away, but my words will never pass away.

The Unknown Day and Hour

"But concerning that day or hour no one knows—not even the angels in heaven nor the Son—except the Father. Watch out! Be alert, because you do not know when the time is! It is like a man away on a journey, who left his house and gave his slaves authority—to each one his work—and to the doorkeeper he gave orders that he should be on the alert. Therefore be on the alert, for you do not know when the master of the house is coming—whether in the evening, or at midnight, or when the rooster crows, or early in the morning—lest he arrive suddenly and find you sleeping. And what I say to you, I say to everyone: Be on the alert!"

Discussion Questions

1. What is the parable of the Fig Tree?

    Response: Reread Mark 13:28–30. The parable's lesson is summarized in v. 28: The appearance of one thing (the branch sprouts leaves) assures us of the next thing that will come (the arrival of summer).

2. Why is the parable of the Fig Tree mentioned here?

    Response: The parable of the Fig Tree reminds us that when the tribulation comes, it means that the return of Christ is near (v. 29).

3. How does this relate to our Advent preparation?

    Response: We celebrate the season of Advent because it reminds us to be attentive and watch for the return of Christ. This passage in Mark includes two key reminders for us: First, it reminds us that Jesus told his followers what sorts of things would happen to indicate his return was near. Second, it reminds us that even then, the timing of his return is a mystery to us. Because we know he is coming—but do not know when—we should be prepared for his return. We will know it when it happens, not before, so we should be ready at all times.

WEEK TWO: Anticipation

Anticipation and preparation go together. If we do not anticipate that something will happen, chances are that we will not prepare for it either.

Anticipating Christ's return involves believing it will happen. It involves remembering what was foretold about him. As Christ was prophesied to come as a babe to Bethlehem (and to die upon the cross), so he is prophesied to come again to take us home.

Anticipating Christ's return prompts us to respond as John did: "Amen! Come, Lord Jesus!" (Rev 22:20).

SUNDAY: Isaiah 40:1-11 (Part 1)

"Comfort; comfort my people," says your God.

"Speak to the heart of Jerusalem, and call to her,

that her compulsory labor is fulfilled, that her sin is paid for,
    that she has received from the hand of Yahweh double for all her sins."

A voice is calling in the wilderness, "Clear the way of Yahweh!
    Make a highway smooth in the desert for our God!

Every valley shall be lifted up,
    and every mountain and hill shall become low,
And the rough ground shall be like a plain,
    and the rugged ground like a valley-plain.
And the glory of Yahweh shall be revealed,
    and all humankind together shall see it,

for the mouth of Yahweh has spoken."

A voice is saying, "Call!"
    And he said, "What shall I call?"
All humankind are grass,
    and all his loyalty is like the flowers of the field.
Grass withers; the flower withers
when the breath of Yahweh blows on it.
    Surely the people are grass.
Grass withers; the flower withers,
    but the word of our God will stand forever.

Get yourself up to a high mountain, Zion, bringer
of good news!
    Lift up your voice with strength, Jerusalem,
    bringer of good news!
Lift it up; you must not fear!
    Say to the cities of Judah, "Here is your God!"
Look! The Lord Yahweh comes with strength,
    and his arm rules for him.
Look! His reward is with him,
    and his recompense in his presence.

He will feed his flock like a shepherd;
    he will gather the lambs in his arm,
and he will carry them in his bosom;
    he will lead those who nurse.

Discussion Questions

1. What did the Lord (Yahweh) do in Isaiah 40:1–2?

   Response: He extends comfort to his people by paying double what is required to cover the peoples' sin. This is a way of saying that what is paid is more than enough to easily cover the debt of sin.

2. What is happening with the mountains and hills and valleys in Isaiah 40:3–5?

   Response: The voice in verse 3 calls for a smooth highway for God. Verse 4 tells how it happens: how the mountains and other high things are leveled and how the valleys and other low things are lifted up. Verse 5 indicates that the glory of the Lord (Yahweh) will be revealed and will be seen by all.

3. How does this relate to our anticipation of Christ's return?

   Response: The God who forgives sin will come in power and glory. Those who love him and belong to him should look forward to his return.

MONDAY: Isaiah 40:1-11 (Part 2)

"Comfort; comfort my people," says your God.

"Speak to the heart of Jerusalem, and call to her,

that her compulsory labor is fulfilled, that her sin
is paid for,
> that she has received from the hand of Yahweh
> double for all her sins."

A voice is calling in the wilderness, "Clear the way
of Yahweh!
> Make a highway smooth in the desert for our
> God!
Every valley shall be lifted up,
> and every mountain and hill shall become low,
And the rough ground shall be like a plain,
> and the rugged ground like a valley-plain.
And the glory of Yahweh shall be revealed,
> and all humankind together shall see it,

for the mouth of Yahweh has spoken."

A voice is saying, "Call!"
> And he said, "What shall I call?"
All humankind are grass,
> and all his loyalty is like the flowers of the field.
Grass withers; the flower withers
when the breath of Yahweh blows on it.
> Surely the people are grass.

Grass withers; the flower withers,
  but the word of our God will stand forever.

Get yourself up to a high mountain, Zion, bringer
of good news!
  Lift up your voice with strength, Jerusalem,
  bringer of good news!
Lift it up; you must not fear!
  Say to the cities of Judah, "Here is your God!"
Look! The Lord Yahweh comes with strength,
  and his arm rules for him.
Look! His reward is with him,
  and his recompense in his presence.
He will feed his flock like a shepherd;
  he will gather the lambs in his arm,
and he will carry them in his bosom;
  he will lead those who nurse.

Discussion Questions

1. Isaiah 40:8, about the grass and flower withering, is well known (see 1 Pet 1:24). What do we learn about that saying in this passage?

Response: We learn that people are like the grass and the loyalty of people is like a flower (v. 6). Just as grass and flowers wither or fade, people and their loyalty to God wither and fade. Despite this, God's word never withers—it will stand.

2. What is the role of Jerusalem, and what is the message it brings (Isa 40:9–11)?

Response: The role of Jerusalem, also known as Zion, is the "bringer of good news" (v. 9). Its message is the presentation of God, who "comes with strength" (v. 10), brings his reward (v. 10), and will take care of his flock (his people; v. 11).

3. How does this relate to our anticipation of Christ's return?

Response: Despite the withering and fading of his people and their loyalty, God will remain true to his word and will return in power to care for them. This sure promise of his return leads to anticipation of his arrival.

TUESDAY: Psalm 85 (Part 1)

O Yahweh, you favored your land.
You restored the fortunes of Jacob.
You took away the guilt of your people;
you covered all their sin. *Selah*
You withdrew all your wrath;
you turned from your burning anger.
Restore us, O God of our salvation,
and annul your vexation with us.
Will you be angry against us forever?

Will you prolong your anger generation after
generation?
Will you not again revive us,
that your people might rejoice in you?
Show us, O Yahweh, your loyal love,
and grant us your salvation.
I will hear what God, Yahweh, will speak,
because he will speak peace
to his people, even his faithful ones,
but let them not return to folly.
Surely his salvation is near for those who fear him,
that glory may abide in our land.
Loyal love and faithfulness will meet one another;
righteousness and peace will kiss.
Faithfulness will sprout from the ground,
and righteousness will look down from heaven.
Yes, Yahweh will give what is good,
and our land will give its produce.
Righteousness will go before him,
and it will make his steps a pathway.

Discussion Questions

1. In Psalm 85:1–3, the psalmist (the person who wrote this psalm) is remembering Yahweh's past actions. What did he do?

   Response: The Lord restored Jacob (Israel). This is probably a reference to Israel's return under Moses and Joshua to the promised land. In particular, the wrath and anger of God against Israel is removed.

2. In vv. 4-7, the psalmist makes requests of Yahweh. What are these requests?

Response: The psalmist asks for Israel to be restored again. He acknowledges that God is angry with him and his people. Still, he asks for the love of God to be shown to them again and for them to be restored to their place with God.

3. How does this relate to our anticipation of Christ's return?

Response: In this passage, we see that the psalmist's separation from God leads the psalmist to long for restoration—and this hope for restoration is anticipation for God's return.

WEDNESDAY: Psalm 85 (Part 2)

> O Yahweh, you favored your land.
> You restored the fortunes of Jacob.
> You took away the guilt of your people;
> you covered all their sin. *Selah*
> You withdrew all your wrath;
> you turned from your burning anger.
> Restore us, O God of our salvation,
> and annul your vexation with us.

Will you be angry against us forever?
Will you prolong your anger generation after
generation?
Will you not again revive us,
that your people might rejoice in you?
Show us, O Yahweh, your loyal love,
and grant us your salvation.
I will hear what God, Yahweh, will speak,
because he will speak peace
to his people, even his faithful ones,
but let them not return to folly.
Surely his salvation is near for those who fear him,
that glory may abide in our land.
Loyal love and faithfulness will meet one another;
righteousness and peace will kiss.
Faithfulness will sprout from the ground,
and righteousness will look down from heaven.
Yes, Yahweh will give what is good,
and our land will give its produce.
Righteousness will go before him,
and it will make his steps a pathway.

Discussion Questions

1. Recall questions one and two from yesterday's reading
   regarding what God did and what the psalmist asked.
   Would you make any similar requests on behalf of
   your family, church, or others?

   Response: Talk with your family.

2. What will the Lord (Yahweh) say (v. 8), and what is the psalmist's response (vv. 9–13)?

Response: The Lord (Yahweh) will speak peace to his people. He will return to them, and restore them. The response is an expression of faith in what the Lord will say and trust that it will occur.

3. How does this relate to our anticipation of Christ's return?

Response: When we are faithful to our belief in his return, we know it will happen. Knowing he will return means we can rest confidently and eagerly anticipate his arrival.

THURSDAY: 2 Peter 3:8-15

Now, dear friends, do not let this one thing escape your notice, that one day with the Lord is like a thousand years, and a thousand years is like one day. The Lord is not delaying the promise, as some consider slowness, but is being patient toward you, because he does not want any to perish, but all to come to repentance. But the day of the Lord will come like a thief, in which the heavens will disappear with a rushing noise, and the celestial bodies will be destroyed by being burned up, and the earth and the deeds done on it will be disclosed. Because all these things are being destroyed in this way, what sort of people must you be in holy behavior and godliness, while waiting for and hastening the coming of the day of God, because of which the heavens will be destroyed by being burned up and the celestial bodies will melt as they are consumed by heat! But according to his promise, we are waiting for new heavens and a new earth in which righteousness resides.

Therefore, dear friends, because you are waiting for these things, make every effort to be found at peace, spotless and unblemished in him. And regard the patience of our Lord as salvation, just as also our dear brother Paul wrote to you, according to the wisdom that was given to him.

Discussion Questions

1. What does 2 Peter 3:8–15 tell us about the timing of the Lord's return?

   Response: The Lord's conception of time is not like our conception of time (v. 8). The timing will be a surprise to us when he comes (v. 10).

YEAR B: Advent Readings

2. What sorts of things will happen on the day of the Lord's return?

Response: Big things will happen—destruction of the skies and the stars and the earth (v. 10, 12). God will give a new heavens and earth. On that day, the deeds of his people will be revealed (v. 10) and their sin destroyed (v. 11). The new heavens and earth will bring righteousness with them, and his people will be restored.

3. How does this relate to our anticipation of Christ's return?

Response: Complete restoration with God results from his coming. Because of this, we anticipate his arrival—and our first reminder is by remembering his coming as a baby to Bethlehem.

FRIDAY: Mark 1:1-8 (Part 1)

The beginning of the gospel of Jesus Christ. Just as it is written in the prophet Isaiah,

> "Behold, I am sending my messenger before your face,
> who will prepare your way,
> the voice of one shouting in the wilderness,

'Prepare the way of the Lord,
make straight his paths!' "

John was there baptizing in the wilderness, proclaiming a baptism of repentance for the forgiveness of sins. And all the Judean region and all the inhabitants of Jerusalem went out to him and were being baptized by him in the Jordan River, confessing their sins. And John was dressed in camel's hair and a belt made of leather around his waist, and he ate locusts and wild honey. And he was preaching, saying, "One who is more powerful than I is coming after me, of whom I am not worthy to bend down and untie the strap of his sandals. I baptized you with water, but he will baptize you with the Holy Spirit."

Discussion Questions

1. The quotation in Mark 1:2–3 is from Isaiah 40:3. We looked at Isaiah 40 earlier this week, on Sunday and Monday. What did we learn about how it relates to our anticipation of Christ's return?

Response: Preparing for the Lord is part of anticipating his arrival.

2. Mark 1:1 mentions "the gospel of Jesus Christ." What is the gospel of Jesus Christ?

Response: The Greek word translated "gospel" means "good news." It indicates favorable information about an event or person. In the New Testament, "gospel" has to do with Jesus and the reason for his coming— his advent—and the good news it is for those who follow him.

3. How does this relate to our anticipation of Christ's return?

Response: Mark's Gospel opens by reminding us of Isaiah's call to prepare the way of the Lord. In our anticipation of Christ's return, we too should prepare our hearts and minds so we can live in anticipation of his coming.

SATURDAY: Mark 1:1-8 (Part 2)

The beginning of the gospel of Jesus Christ. Just as it is written in the prophet Isaiah,

"Behold, I am sending my messenger before your face,
who will prepare your way,
the voice of one shouting in the wilderness,

'Prepare the way of the Lord,
make straight his paths!' "

John was there baptizing in the wilderness, proclaiming a baptism of repentance for the forgiveness of sins. And all the Judean region and all the inhabitants of Jerusalem went out to him and were being baptized by him in the Jordan River, confessing their sins. And John was dressed in camel's hair and a belt made of leather around his waist, and he ate locusts and wild honey. And he was preaching, saying, "One who is more powerful than I is coming after me, of whom I am not worthy to bend down and untie the strap of his sandals. I baptized you with water, but he will baptize you with the Holy Spirit."

Discussion Questions

1. Why is John the Baptist mentioned after the quotation of Isaiah 40:3?

   Response: The ministry of John the Baptist was "preparing the way" for the ministry of Jesus. John preached that someone "more powerful" was coming after him, someone who would baptize not with water but with the Holy Spirit. This is good news, indeed!

2. John proclaimed "a baptism of repentance for the forgiveness of sins." What is that?

Response: John baptized as a symbol. Baptism wasn't new—it was a religious practice that signified purification. In John's context, it wasn't just a simple washing to cleanse oneself for a particular religious ceremony. For John, baptism was tied to repentance and forgiveness. It indicated that one was preparing for the Messiah to come.

3. How does this relate to our anticipation of Christ's return?

Response: John's baptism was part of the preparation for Jesus' first coming, his first advent. Remembering what he preached and how people responded to his message can help us to better prepare for and anticipate Jesus' second coming.

WEEK THREE: Joy

Preparation and anticipation have focused our thoughts and actions on the arrival of Christ. As this arrival draws closer, a natural consequence is joy. When the thing we have been waiting for gets closer and closer, joy increases.

When I was a boy, my dad was in the Navy. There were times he was away from home for months. We wrote letters—there was no email then—to keep in touch. If he was in port, he would call us. But as the day of his homecoming drew closer, our whole family grew excited. The joy started before he came home, when months turned to weeks, weeks turned to days, and days turned to hours.

Joy is a natural part of anticipating Christ's return as we consider what he has accomplished for us and what he will accomplish for us. Our Savior lives! Our King is returning! And he will take us home.

SUNDAY: Isaiah 64:1-4, 8-11 (Part 1)

> Would that you would tear the heavens and come down;
>> the mountains would quake before you,
> as fire kindles brushwood,
>> the fire causes water to boil,
> to make your name known to your adversaries,

that the nations might tremble from your
presence.

When you did terrible deeds which we did not
expect, you came down;
  the mountains quaked because of your
  presence.

And since ancient times they have not heard,
  have not listened,
no eye has seen a God except you;
  he acts for the one who waits for him...

Yet now Yahweh, you are our father;
  we are the clay and you are our potter,
  and we all are the work of your hand.

You must not be exceedingly angry, Yahweh,
  and you must not remember iniquity forever!

Look! Behold, now! We all are your people!

Your holy cities have become a wilderness;
  Zion has become a wilderness, Jerusalem a
  desolation.
Our holy and beautiful temple, where our
ancestors praised you has been burned by fire,
  and all our precious objects have become ruins.

Discussion Questions

1. Who is "you" in Isaiah 64:1–4?

   Response: "You" is the Lord (Yahweh).

2. What is he being asked to do? And why?

   Response: He is being asked to come down from heaven and intercede for his people, to frighten their enemies so that they, too, will respect the God of Israel.

3. How does this relate to joy during the Advent season?

   Response: The coming of the Lord—and, in this case, his intercession on their behalf—brings joy to his people.

MONDAY: Isaiah 64:1-4, 8-11 (Part 2)

Would that you would tear the heavens and come
down;
     the mountains would quake before you,
as fire kindles brushwood,
     the fire causes water to boil,
to make your name known to your adversaries,
     that the nations might tremble from your
     presence.

When you did terrible deeds which we did not
expect, you came down;
     the mountains quaked because of your presence.

And since ancient times they have not heard,
> have not listened,
no eye has seen a God except you;
> he acts for the one who waits for him ...

Yet now Yahweh, you are our father;
> we are the clay and you are our potter,
> and we all are the work of your hand.

You must not be exceedingly angry, Yahweh,
> and you must not remember iniquity forever!

Look! Behold, now! We all are your people!

Your holy cities have become a wilderness;
> Zion has become a wilderness, Jerusalem a
> desolation.
Our holy and beautiful temple, where our
ancestors praised you has been burned by fire,
> and all our precious objects have become ruins.

Discussion Questions

1. What is the relationship between the Lord (Yahweh) and the people?

   Response: The people claim the Lord (Yahweh) as father (v. 8). The image of clay (the people) and a potter (Yahweh) is used to reinforce this.

2. Why would Yahweh be angry?

Response: Because the land is in shambles (vv. 10–11). The holy cities are empty. Jerusalem is desolate. And the temple, the very house of the Lord, has been destroyed.

3. How does this relate to joy during the Advent season?

Response: The people expect the Lord to return and bring salvation to the land. They call upon him to rebuild the temple, to annihilate their enemies, and to exalt his people to their proper place. Though the situation is dire, they rejoice at the thought of his return, which will restore the world to how it should be. We should exhibit the same joy at the thought of his second coming.

TUESDAY: Psalm 126

When Yahweh restored the fortunes of Zion,
we were like dreamers.
Then our mouth was filled with laughter,
and our tongue with rejoicing.
Then they said among the nations,
"Yahweh has done great things for these people."
Yahweh has done great things for us;
we are glad.
Restore, O Yahweh, our fortunes
like the streams in the Negeb.
Those who sow with tears

shall reap with rejoicing.
He who diligently goes out with weeping,
carrying the seed bag,
shall certainly come in with rejoicing,
carrying his sheaves.

Discussion Questions

1. Why are the people in the psalm rejoicing?

   Response: The people are remembering when Zion (Jerusalem) has been restored (v. 1).

2. What are the people mentioned in the psalm asking?

   Response: The people are requesting their restoration, like Jerusalem had been restored in former days (v. 1, 4). When they are restored, there will be great rejoicing. They are now sowing with tears, but when the time comes to reap, they will reap with joy (v. 5).

3. How does this relate to joy during the Advent season?

   Response: In the same way that those in the psalm remembered the past restoration of Jerusalem to find joy in their future restoration with the Lord, those who are his should also rejoice as the second coming of Christ approaches.

WEDNESDAY: Luke 1:46-55

And Mary said,

> "My soul exalts the Lord,
>> and my spirit has rejoiced greatly in
> God my Savior,
> because he has looked upon the humble
> state of his female slave,
>> for behold, from now on all
> generations will consider me blessed,
> because the Mighty One has done great
> things for me,
>> and holy is his name.
> And his mercy is for generation after
> generation
>> to those who fear him.
> He has done a mighty deed with his arm;
>> he has dispersed the proud in the
> thoughts of their hearts.
> He has brought down rulers from their
> thrones,
>> and has exalted the lowly.
> He has filled those who are hungry with
> good things,
>> and those who are rich he has sent
> away empty-handed.
> He has helped Israel his servant,
>> remembering his mercy,

> just as he spoke to our fathers,
>> to Abraham and to his descendants
> forever."

Discussion Questions

1. Why is Mary rejoicing?

   Response: Mary is rejoicing because despite her "humble state" (v. 48), she has been blessed by the Lord. The mercy of the Lord that she experienced is overwhelming and undeserved (vv. 49-50), and she praises his name because of it.

2. How does this relate to joy during the Advent season?

   Response: The mercy we receive as a result of Jesus' first coming is similarly overwhelming and undeserved—and we should rejoice because of it! It also leads us to rejoice all the more at the thought of his second coming.

THURSDAY: 1 Thessalonians 5:16-24

> Rejoice always, pray constantly, give thanks in everything; for this is the will of God for you in Christ Jesus. Do not quench the Spirit. Do not despise prophecies, but examine all things; hold fast to what is good. Abstain from every form of evil. Now may the God of peace

himself sanctify you completely, and may your spirit and soul and body be kept complete, blameless at the coming of our Lord Jesus Christ. The one who calls you is faithful, who also will do this.

Discussion Questions

1. What sorts of things does Paul tell the Thessalonians to do?

   Response: Paul tells the Thessalonians to:

   - Rejoice always (v. 16)
   - Pray constantly (v. 17)
   - Give thanks (v. 18)
   - Do not quench the Spirit (v. 19)
   - Do not despise prophecies (v. 20)
   - Hold fast to what is good (v. 21)
   - Stay away from every form of evil (v. 22)

2. What is Paul's wish for the Thessalonians?

   Response: Paul's prayer for the Thessalonians is that they will be sanctified (v. 23; see also 1 Thess 4:3) and that they will be ready for the return of the Lord. When the guidelines he gives in vv. 16–22 are present in their lives, the Thessalonians show their progress toward being ready.

3. How does this relate to joy during the Advent season?

Response: The Lord is coming back, and he is faithful. He will prepare us for his return. When we recognize evidence of his preparation, we should rejoice and remember that he will return.

FRIDAY: John 1:6-8, 19-28 (Part 1)

A man came, sent from God, whose name was John. This one came for a witness, in order that he could testify about the light, so that all would believe through him. That one was not the light, but came in order that he could testify about the light. ...

And this is the testimony of John, when the Jews sent priests and Levites from Jerusalem so that they could ask him, "Who are you?" And he confessed—and he did not deny, and confessed—"I am not the Christ!" And they asked him, "Then who are you? Are you Elijah?" And he said, "I am not!" "Are you the Prophet?" And he answered, "No!" Then they said to him, "Who are you, so that we can give an answer to those who sent us? What do you say about yourself?"

He said,

"I am 'the voice of one crying out in the

wilderness,

"Make straight the way of the Lord," '

just as Isaiah the prophet said." (And they had been sent from the Pharisees.) And they asked him and said to him, "Why then are you baptizing, if you are not the Christ, nor Elijah, nor the Prophet?"

John answered them, saying, "I baptize with water. In your midst stands one whom you do not know—the one who comes after me, of whom I am not worthy to untie the strap of his sandal!" These things took place in Bethany on the other side of the Jordan, where John was baptizing.

Discussion Questions

1. Why was John sent? And who is "the light"?

   Response: John was sent to tell people about "the light" (vv. 7-8). The light is Jesus Christ. John's job was to tell the world of the coming of the Messiah, Jesus.

2. Why did the people confuse John with "the Christ" (the Messiah, Jesus) and Elijah?

   Response: John was doing amazing things, things that caused people to think he was the Messiah (v. 20). There were also prophecies that Elijah would return prior to the return of the Lord (see Mal 4:5). John's appearance even reminded some of Elijah (v. 21; see 2 Kgs 1:8).

3. How does this relate to joy during the Advent season?

Response: The beginning of Jesus' earthly ministry was announced by John the Baptist. It was not a secret. The second advent of Jesus, his triumphal return, will occur. As it gets close, there will be signs of his coming. We should rejoice in the expectation of seeing them.

SATURDAY: John 1:6-8, 19-28 (Part 2)

A man came, sent from God, whose name was John. This one came for a witness, in order that he could testify about the light, so that all would believe through him. That one was not the light, but came in order that he could testify about the light. ...

And this is the testimony of John, when the Jews sent priests and Levites from Jerusalem so that they could ask him, "Who are you?" And he confessed—and he did not deny, and confessed—"I am not the Christ!" And they asked him, "Then who are you? Are you Elijah?" And he said, "I am not!" "Are you the Prophet?" And he answered, "No!" Then they said to him, "Who are you, so that we can give

an answer to those who sent us? What do you
say about yourself?"

He said,

> "I am 'the voice of one crying out in the
> wilderness,
>> "Make straight the way of the Lord," '

just as Isaiah the prophet said." (And they had
been sent from the Pharisees.) And they asked
him and said to him, "Why then are you baptizing, if you are not the Christ, nor Elijah, nor
the Prophet?"

John answered them, saying, "I baptize
with water. In your midst stands one whom
you do not know—the one who comes after
me, of whom I am not worthy to untie the
strap of his sandal!" These things took place
in Bethany on the other side of the Jordan,
where John was baptizing.

Discussion Questions

1. Who did John say that he was?

Response: John replied to this question by quoting
Isaiah 40:3. We looked at Isaiah 40 on Sunday and
Monday of Week 2. In Isaiah 40:3–5, a voice tells the
earth to get ready for the arrival of the Lord, and in
response the whole earth prepares. Here, John claims

that he is that voice (v. 22–23; also in Matt 3:3; Mark 1:3; Luke 3:4).

2. Why did John baptize (vv. 25–27)?

Response: Mark 1:4–5, which we examined on Saturday of Week 2, talks about John's baptism. John's baptism was about repentance and forgiveness of sins; it was not a simple ceremonial practice of cleansing oneself. John baptized to prepare people for the Messiah, Jesus.

3. How does this relate to joy during the Advent season?

Response: John announced the coming of the Messiah. His message was one of preparation. We only prepare for things that we expect to happen, so we should be joyful as we prepare for the return of the Lord.

WEEK FOUR: Incarnation

Incarnation is a mysterious thing that we cannot fully comprehend: How the Son of the living God took on flesh to be like us, to save us. Though we do not understand how it happened, we can, like the author of Hebrews, appreciate it greatly:

> Therefore, since the children share in blood and flesh, he also in like manner shared in these same things, in order that through death he could destroy the one who has the power of death, that is, the devil, and could set free these who through fear of death were subject to slavery throughout all their lives. For surely he is not concerned with angels, but he is concerned with the descendants of Abraham. Therefore he was obligated to be made like his brothers in all respects, in order that he could become a merciful and faithful high priest in the things relating to God, in order to make atonement for the sins of the people. For in that which he himself suffered when he was tempted, he is able to help those who are tempted (Hebrews 2:14-18).

SUNDAY: 2 Samuel 7:1-16 (Part 1)

It happened that the king settled in his house. (Now Yahweh had given rest to him from all his enemies all around.) And the king said to Nathan the prophet, "Look, please, I am living in a house of cedar, but the ark of God is staying in the middle of the tent." Nathan said to the king, "Go and do all that is in your heart, for Yahweh is with you." But it happened that night the word of Yahweh came to Nathan, saying, "Go and tell my servant David, 'Thus says Yahweh: "Are you the one to build for me a house for my dwelling? For I have not dwelt in a house from the day I brought up the Israelites from Egypt until this day; rather, I was going about in a tent and in a tabernacle. In all of my going about among all the Israelites, did I speak a word with one of the tribes of Israel whom I commanded to shepherd my people Israel, saying, 'Why did you not build me a cedar house?' " ' So then, thus you shall say to my servant David, 'Thus says Yahweh of hosts, "I took you from the pasture from following the sheep to be a leader over my people, over Israel, and I have been with you everywhere you went. I have cut off all of your enemies from in front of you, and I will make a great name for you, as the name of the great ones who are on the earth. I will make a place for my people Israel, and I will plant them so that they can dwell in their own place. They will not tremble any longer, and the children of wickedness will not afflict them again, as in the former days. In the manner that I appointed judges over my people Israel, I will give you rest from all your enemies. And Yahweh declares to you that Yahweh will build a house for you. When your days are full and you lie down with your ancestors, I will raise up your offspring after you who will go out from your body, and I will establish his kingdom. He will build a house for my name, and I will establish the throne of his kingdom forever. I will be a father to him, and he will be a son for me, whom I will punish when he does wrong, with a rod of men and with blows of human beings. But my loyal love shall not depart from him as I took it from Saul, whom I removed from before you. Your house and your kingdom shall endure forever before you; your throne shall be established forever." ' "

Discussion Questions

1. Why did David want to build a temple for Yahweh?

Response: David lived in an extravagant, luxurious house, and he saw that Yahweh's presence was in a tabernacle—a tent (vv. 1–3). David wanted Yahweh's presence to be in a place worthy of his glory.

2. Why did Yahweh reject David's wish to build a temple (vv. 4–13)?

Response: David's desire wasn't wrong, but Yahweh was already present in the manner he had specified to the Israelites when they were wandering in the desert. Yahweh first made a place for his people (v. 10), and this was done through David. After his people had a home, Yahweh would *then* allow a more permanent structure for his own presence.

3. How does this passage show that the incarnation is important to remember during Advent?

Response: This passage illustrates Yahweh's love for his people. He provides for them, and his ultimate provision is Jesus, the Messiah, who is God in the flesh for us. As David was motivated and excited by the thought of Yahweh's presence being among Israel, so we should be excited by the return of his presence among us in Jesus.

MONDAY: 2 Samuel 7:1-16 (Part 2)

It happened that the king settled in his house. (Now Yahweh had given rest to him from all his enemies all around.) And the king said to

Nathan the prophet, "Look, please, I am living in a house of cedar, but the ark of God is staying in the middle of the tent." Nathan said to the king, "Go and do all that is in your heart, for Yahweh is with you." But it happened that night the word of Yahweh came to Nathan, saying, "Go and tell my servant David, 'Thus says Yahweh: "Are you the one to build for me a house for my dwelling? For I have not dwelt in a house from the day I brought up the Israelites from Egypt until this day; rather, I was going about in a tent and in a tabernacle. In all of my going about among all the Israelites, did I speak a word with one of the tribes of Israel whom I commanded to shepherd my people Israel, saying, 'Why did you not build me a cedar house?' " ' So then, thus you shall say to my servant David, 'Thus says Yahweh of hosts, "I took you from the pasture from following the sheep to be a leader over my people, over Israel, and I have been with you everywhere you went. I have cut off all of your enemies from in front of you, and I will make a great name for you, as the name of the great ones who are on the earth. I will make a place for my people Israel, and I will plant them so that they can dwell in their own place. They will not tremble any longer, and the children of wickedness will not afflict them again, as in the former days. In the manner that I appointed judges over my people Israel, I will give you rest from all your enemies. And Yahweh declares to you that Yahweh will build a house for you. When your days are full and you lie down with your ancestors, I will raise up your offspring after you who will go out from your body, and I will establish his kingdom. He will build a house for my name, and I will establish the throne of his kingdom forever. I will be a father to him, and he will be a son for me, whom I will punish when he does wrong, with a rod of men and with blows of human beings. But my loyal love shall not depart from him as I took it from Saul, whom I removed from before you. Your house and your kingdom shall endure forever before you; your throne shall be established forever." ' "

Discussion Questions

1. What does Yahweh promise to do in this passage?

   Response: Many of Yahweh's promises in this passage are indicated by "I will" or "I shall." These include:

   - "I will make a great name for you" (v. 9)
   - "I will make a place for my people" (v. 10)
   - "I will give you rest from all your enemies" (v. 11)

- "Yahweh will build a house for you" (v. 11)
- "I will raise up your offspring ... and I will establish his kingdom" (v. 12)
- "He [David's son, Solomon] will build a house for my name" (v. 13)
- "I will be a father to him, and he will be a son for me" (v. 14)
- "My loyal love shall not depart from him" (v. 15)
- "Your house and your kingdom shall endure forever before you; your throne shall be established forever" (v. 16)

2. How does this passage show that the incarnation is important to remember during Advent?

Response: In this passage, Yahweh makes promises to David that his kingdom will endure forever. This is a promise that is fully and finally realized in the Messiah, Jesus, who is also called the "Son of David" (see Luke 1:32, 69). The Messiah, the incarnate one, is the Son of David, the fulfillment of this promise. When we see the promise made, and we know the one who made it is trustworthy, we should be filled with joy to see its fulfillment coming closer.

TUESDAY: Luke 1:46-55

And Mary said,

> "My soul exalts the Lord,
>> and my spirit has rejoiced greatly in
> God my Savior,
> because he has looked upon the humble
> state of his female slave,
>> for behold, from now on all
> generations will consider me blessed,
> because the Mighty One has done great
> things for me,
>> and holy is his name.
> And his mercy is for generation after
> generation
>> to those who fear him.
> He has done a mighty deed with his arm;
>> he has dispersed the proud in the
> thoughts of their hearts.
> He has brought down rulers from their
> thrones,
>> and has exalted the lowly.
> He has filled those who are hungry with
> good things,
>> and those who are rich he has sent
> away empty-handed.
> He has helped Israel his servant,
>> remembering his mercy,

just as he spoke to our fathers,
     to Abraham and to his descendants
forever."

Discussion Questions

1. We looked at this passage last week on Wednesday, focusing on joy in Advent. What is mentioned in this passage that is worthy of rejoicing over?

   Response: In this passage, often called "Mary's song," we see that God acts for his people. God protects them, preserves them, and extends mercy to them. These things should cause us to rejoice.

2. Why is Abraham mentioned in v. 55?

   Response: The things that God promised Abraham are coming true. This not only points to Abraham but also to the promises God made to David that we read about yesterday and the day before in 2 Samuel 7:15-16. The promise that David's house would endure forever will be kept in Mary's child, the incarnate God—fully God and fully man.

3. How does this passage show that the incarnation is important to remember during Advent?

   Response: God will keep his promises—all will be realized in Jesus, born of Mary, God in the flesh. This is precious because it means we have hope.

WEDNESDAY: Psalm 89:1-4, 19-26 (Part 1)

I will sing forever of Yahweh's acts of loyal love.
From generation to generation
I will make known your faithfulness with my
mouth.
For I say, "Forever your loyal love is built up.
The heavens you have established with your
faithfulness in them."
"I made a covenant with my chosen one;
I swore an oath to David my servant:
'I will establish your descendants forever,
and I will build up your throne from generation to
generation.'" *Selah* ...

Formerly you spoke in a vision
to your faithful ones, and said,
"I have bestowed help on a mighty man;
I have exalted one chosen from the people.
I have found David, my servant.
With my holy oil I have anointed him,
with whom my hand will be steadfast.
Surely my arm will strengthen him.
The enemy will not deceive him,
and no evil man will afflict him.
But I will crush his adversaries before him,
and I will strike those who hate him.
And so my faithfulness
and my loyal love will be with him,

and in my name his horn will rise up.
And I will set his hand on the sea
and his right hand on the rivers.
He will call out to me, 'You are my Father,
my God, and the rock of my salvation.' "

Discussion Questions

1. What do verses 1–4 say about the promises God made to David?

   Response: They show that these promises were important and were remembered (see 2 Sam 7:15–16). This psalm is essentially a song about these promises. It wasn't written by David but by one of his singers named Ethan (1 Chr 15:16–19; see also 1 Kgs 4:31). These promises were known by more people than just David, and people who knew them rejoiced and sang in their knowledge of these promises.

2. How does this passage show that the incarnation is important to remember during Advent?

   Response: These promises are joyous! Their fulfillment is in Jesus, the Messiah. In the New Testament, Jesus was called the Son of David, an indication of this fulfillment. The arrival of the Son of David at the first advent was precious. His arrival at the second advent will be more so to those who are his.

THURSDAY: Psalm 89:1-4, 19-26 (Part 2)

I will sing forever of Yahweh's acts of loyal love.
From generation to generation
I will make known your faithfulness with my
mouth.
For I say, "Forever your loyal love is built up.
The heavens you have established with your
faithfulness in them."
"I made a covenant with my chosen one;
I swore an oath to David my servant:
'I will establish your descendants forever,
and I will build up your throne from generation to
generation.'" *Selah* ...

Formerly you spoke in a vision
to your faithful ones, and said,
"I have bestowed help on a mighty man;
I have exalted one chosen from the people.
I have found David, my servant.
With my holy oil I have anointed him,
with whom my hand will be steadfast.
Surely my arm will strengthen him.
The enemy will not deceive him,
and no evil man will afflict him.
But I will crush his adversaries before him,
and I will strike those who hate him.
And so my faithfulness
and my loyal love will be with him,

and in my name his horn will rise up.
And I will set his hand on the sea
and his right hand on the rivers.
He will call out to me, 'You are my Father,
my God, and the rock of my salvation.' "

Discussion Questions

1. What does God promise David?

Response: God makes several promises (vv. 20–25):

- God's hand will be steadfast (God will always be with David; v. 21)
- God will strengthen him (v. 21)
- God will destroy his enemies (v. 22)
- God's loyal love will always be with him (v. 24)
- God will give him dominion (v. 24–25)

2. How does this passage show that the incarnation is important to remember during Advent?

Response: When these promises to David are completely fulfilled, God's kingdom will be fully established. This will be done through the incarnate God, Jesus Christ. Without him, it will not happen. Because of him, we will be fully reconciled with God.

FRIDAY: Titus 2:11-14

For the grace of God has appeared, bringing salvation to all people, training us in order that, denying impiety and worldly desires, we may live self-controlled and righteously and godly in the present age, looking forward to the blessed hope and the glorious appearing of our great God and Savior Jesus Christ, who gave himself for us, in order that he might redeem us from all lawlessness and purify for himself a people for his own possession, zealous for good deeds.

Discussion Questions

1. What (or who) is "the grace of God" that appeared?

   Response: The grace of God, which brings salvation, is here personified as Jesus Christ (v. 11). It is through Jesus that God's grace is made available.

2. What has he done for us?

   Response: The grace of God:

   - helps us live "self-controlled and righteously and godly" (v. 12)
   - points us to the glorious return of Jesus (v. 13)
   - redeems us and purifies us through Jesus (v. 14)

3. How does this passage show that the incarnation is important to remember during Advent?

Response: Jesus Christ is God and Savior (v. 13) and it is through him that we are redeemed. We were separated from God by sin; Jesus redeems us from that sin and purifies us (v. 14). He brings us back to God. He removes the separation. He is our Savior, the one who saves us.

SATURDAY: Luke 1:26-33

Now in the sixth month, the angel Gabriel was sent from God to a town of Galilee named Nazareth, to a virgin legally promised in marriage to a man named Joseph of the house of David. And the name of the virgin was Mary. And he came to her and said, "Greetings, favored one! The Lord is with you." But she was greatly perplexed at the statement, and was pondering what sort of greeting this might be. And the angel said to her,

>"Do not be afraid, Mary, for you have found favor with God.
>And behold, you will conceive in the womb and will give birth to a son,
>>and you will call his name Jesus.

This one will be great, and he will be
called the Son of the Most High,
    and the Lord God will give him the
throne of his father David.
And he will reign over the house of
Jacob forever,
    and of his kingdom there will be no
end."

Discussion Questions

1. What was the promise that Gabriel gave to Mary?

   Response: Gabriel told Mary that she would give birth
   to a son whose name would be Jesus (v. 31), and that he
   would fulfill promises to David (v. 32) and would reign
   over the "house of Jacob" (Israel) forever (v. 33).

2. Whose throne will be given to Mary's son? Why is
   this important?

   Response: David's throne will be given to Mary's
   son (v. 32). This is important because it shows that
   Jesus is the fulfillment of the promises made to David
   (2 Sam 7:15–16; Psa 89).

3. How does this passage show that the incarnation is
   important to remember during Advent?

   Response: This passage directly ties the promises that
   God made to David with the birth of Jesus. The one
   promised to David is realized in Jesus. His birth to

Mary means that with the first advent of Jesus, the fulfillment of the promise has begun. It points us to the second advent, the return of Jesus, which will be the fulfillment of our hope.

YEAR C
ADVENT READINGS

Year C of the three-year liturgical cycle focuses on Luke for its gospel readings. A selection from Luke 21 reminds us that the Son of Man will come, and that his arrival will not be a surprise for those who are prepared. Zechariah's prayer (Luke 1:68–79) introduces us to the prophetic role of his son, John the Baptist, and Luke 3 opens our eyes to John's ministry announcing the coming of the Messiah. The latter part of Luke 3 points directly toward the Messiah's arrival and how he will come to collect his own people. And the story of Mary's visit with Elizabeth in Luke 1 reminds us, through the in-the-womb response of John the Baptist to Mary's visit, how precious the incarnation really is.

WEEK ONE: Preparation

In this first week of Advent, our goal is to set our minds on what is coming. Remembering and considering prophecies about Christ's second coming is about preparing our minds and our thinking—about setting our minds on what is above. But preparation also involves action. If we are preparing for a hurricane, we don't only watch weather reports to verify that we are in its path—we also prepare the house, store supplies, and create an evacuation plan.

Preparation for the coming of Christ means remembering what we have been told about his coming and actively preparing for his arrival.

SUNDAY: Jeremiah 33:14-16

> "Look, days are coming," declares Yahweh, "and I will fulfill the good promise that I promised to the house of Israel and to the house of Judah. In those days and in that time I will make a branch of righteousness sprout for David, and he will execute justice and righteousness in the land. In those days Judah will be saved, and Jerusalem will dwell safely, and this is what they shall call it: 'Yahweh is our righteousness.'"

Discussion Questions

1. What does the Lord (Yahweh) promise to do?

   Response: Yahweh makes several promises, including:

   - "I will fulfill the good promise that I promised to the house of Israel and to the house of Judah" (v. 14)
   - "I will make a branch of righteousness sprout for David" (v. 15)
   - The righteous branch "will execute justice and righteousness in the land" (v. 15)
   - "Judah will be saved" (v. 16)
   - "Jerusalem will dwell safely" (v. 16)

2. When does he promise to do it?

   Response: This will happen sometime in the future: "days are coming" (v. 14); "in those days" (vv. 15, 16); "in that time" (v. 15). There is also a future component throughout the verses: "I will make sprout," "he will execute" (v. 15), "will be saved," "will dwell safely," "it will be called" (v. 16).

3. How does this relate to our Advent preparation?

   Response: The Lord has promised to do something, and he has promised to do it in the future. This Scripture from Jeremiah may apply to both Christ's first advent (his birth in Bethlehem) and his second advent (his coming return). We are reminded that Christ's first coming was prophesied and it happened. His second coming will surely happen too. We must prepare and be ready.

MONDAY: Psalm 25:1-10 (Part 1)

To you, O Yahweh, I lift up my soul.
O my God, I trust you; let me not be put to shame.
Do not let my enemies exult over me.
Indeed, none who wait for you should be put to shame.
Those who betray without cause should be put to shame.
Make me know your ways, O Yahweh.
Teach me your paths.
Cause me to walk in your truth and teach me,
because you are the God of my salvation.
I await you all day long.
Remember your compassion, O Yahweh,
and your acts of loyal love,
because they are from of old.
Do not remember
the sins of my youth or my transgressions.
According to your loyal love remember me if you will,
for the sake of your goodness, O Yahweh.
Good and right is Yahweh;

therefore he instructs sinners in the way.
He causes the humble to walk in justice,
and teaches the humble his way.
All the paths of Yahweh are loyal love and
faithfulness
for those who keep his covenant and statutes.

Discussion Questions

1. How is David "waiting for" the Lord?

   Response: David lists the following actions:

   - "I lift up my soul" (v. 1)
   - "I trust you," with the expectation that he will "not be put to shame" and that his enemies ultimately will not get the best of him (v. 2)

   David is waiting for the Lord to guide him; he knows that waiting and preparing is better than acting without knowing God's will.

2. How does this relate to our Advent preparation?

   Response: Our preparation may consist of actions similar to David's. We prepare by waiting patiently in expectation. We prepare by learning more about him, by seeking his will. We prepare by knowing why we desire to wait and to seek his will—because he is the God of our salvation. And we prepare by remembering this, and by knowing that our patient waiting in expectation will not be done in vain.

TUESDAY: Psalm 25:1-10 (Part 2)

To you, O Yahweh, I lift up my soul.
O my God, I trust you; let me not be put to shame.
Do not let my enemies exult over me.
Indeed, none who wait for you should be put to shame.
Those who betray without cause should be put to shame.
Make me know your ways, O Yahweh.
Teach me your paths.
Cause me to walk in your truth and teach me,
because you are the God of my salvation.
I await you all day long.
Remember your compassion, O Yahweh,
and your acts of loyal love,
because they are from of old.
Do not remember
the sins of my youth or my transgressions.
According to your loyal love remember me if you will,
for the sake of your goodness, O Yahweh.
Good and right is Yahweh;
therefore he instructs sinners in the way.
He causes the humble to walk in justice,

and teaches the humble his way.
All the paths of Yahweh are loyal love and
faithfulness
for those who keep his covenant and statutes.

Discussion Questions

1. What place does sin have in David's life?

   Response: David does not want "the sins of his youth" (v. 7) to have any part in his life; he wants God to forget them completely. He desires God's mercy, but he knows he deserves God's wrath.

2. What place does God have in David's life?

   Response: David knows that God's way is right, and that following God's path will draw him closer to God through God's steadfast love and faithfulness.

3. How does this relate to our Advent preparation?

   Response: As David models repentance in Psalm 25, so too we should repent of our sins. As David desires God's mercy in Psalm 25, so too we should desire God's mercy. And as David seeks the path of the Lord, so too we should seek his path to prepare for his arrival.

WEDNESDAY: 1 Thessalonians 3:9-13

For what thanks can we repay to God concerning you, because of all the joy with which we rejoice because of you before our God, night and day praying beyond all measure that we may see your face and complete what is lacking in your faith?

Now may our God and Father himself and our Lord Jesus direct our way to you, and may the Lord cause you to increase and to abound in love for one another and for all, just as also we do for you, so that your hearts may be established blameless in holiness before our God and Father at the coming of our Lord Jesus with all his saints.

Discussion Questions

1. What is Paul's prayer for the Thessalonians?

   Response: Paul prays that the needs of the Thessalonians will be met; that he (and those with him) will be able to reconnect with the Thessalonians; and that at the return of Jesus their hearts may be established as "blameless in holiness" (v. 13) before God.

2. How does this relate to our Advent preparation?

   Response: We too should desire for our hearts to be established as blameless in holiness at Christ's return.

We should offer prayers of repentance. We should be led "to increase and to abound in love for one another and for all" (v. 12).

THURSDAY: Luke 21:25-36 (Part 1)

The Arrival of the Son of Man

"And there will be signs in the sun and moon and stars, and on the earth distress of nations in perplexity from the noise of the sea and its surging, people fainting from fear and expectation of what is coming on the inhabited earth, for the powers of the heavens will be shaken. And then they will see the Son of Man arriving in a cloud with power and great glory. But when these things begin to happen, stand up straight and raise your heads, because your redemption is drawing near!"

The Parable of the Fig Tree

And he told them a parable: "Look at the fig tree and all the trees. When they put out foliage, now you see for yourselves and know that by this time the summer is near. So also you, when you see these things happening, know that the kingdom of God is near. Truly I say to you that this generation will never pass away until all things take place! Heaven and earth will pass away, but my words will never pass away.

Be Alert

"But take care for yourselves, lest your hearts are weighed down with dissipation and drunkenness and the worries of daily life, and that day come upon you suddenly like a trap. For it will come upon all who reside on the face of the whole earth. But be alert at all times, praying that you may have strength to escape all these things that are going to happen, and to stand before the Son of Man."

Discussion Questions

1. Who is coming?

   Response: The Son of Man (v. 27) is coming. This refers to Jesus Christ's return.

2. Is there any warning?

   Response: Yes. The text makes clear that we will be aware of his coming before he comes. The important part about this passage isn't the specific things mentioned as preceding Christ's arrival. The important part is that after huge events occur, we have verse 27: "And then they will see the Son of Man." God will get our attention, and we will see and know the return of Christ.

3. How does this relate to our Advent preparation?

Response: In our preparation, we should remember to look for Christ's arrival, knowing that God is faithful and will make Christ's arrival known. In the midst of anticipating his arrival, v. 28 should be a comfort: "But when these things begin to happen, stand up straight and raise your heads, because your redemption is drawing near!"

FRIDAY: Luke 21:25-36 (Part 2)

The Arrival of the Son of Man

"And there will be signs in the sun and moon and stars, and on the earth distress of nations in perplexity from the noise of the sea and its surging, people fainting from fear and expectation of what is coming on the inhabited earth, for the powers of the heavens will be shaken. And then they will see the Son of Man arriving in a cloud with power and great glory. But when these things begin to happen, stand up straight and raise your heads, because your redemption is drawing near!"

The Parable of the Fig Tree

And he told them a parable: "Look at the fig tree and all the trees. When they put out foliage, now you see for yourselves and know that by this time the summer is near. So also you, when you see these things happening, know that the kingdom of God is near. Truly I say to you that this generation will never pass away until all things take place! Heaven and earth will pass away, but my words will never pass away.

Be Alert

"But take care for yourselves, lest your hearts are weighed down with dissipation and drunkenness and the worries of daily life, and that day come upon you suddenly like a trap. For it will come upon all who reside on the face of the whole earth. But be alert at all times, praying that you may have strength to escape all these things that are going to happen, and to stand before the Son of Man."

Discussion Questions

1. What is the main metaphor in the parable of the Fig Tree?

   Response: When fig trees bloom, you know summer is near.

2. What is the lesson we need to learn from this metaphor?

Response: In the same way that blooming fig trees herald the onset of summer, God will make clear when his kingdom is near.

3. How does this relate to our Advent preparation?

Response: This passage (Luke 21:29–33) follows our previous reading (vv. 25–28) and offers support for the lesson learned there—that God will make Christ's return clear to us. The lesson is the same, as v. 31 reminds us: "When you see these things happening, know that the kingdom of God is near."

SATURDAY: Luke 21:25-36 (Part 3)

The Arrival of the Son of Man

"And there will be signs in the sun and moon and stars, and on the earth distress of nations in perplexity from the noise of the sea and its surging, people fainting from fear and expectation of what is coming on the inhabited earth, for the powers of the heavens will be shaken. And then they will see the Son of Man arriving in a cloud with power and great glory. But when these things begin to happen, stand up straight and raise your heads, because your redemption is drawing near!"

The Parable of the Fig Tree

And he told them a parable: "Look at the fig tree and all the trees. When they put out foliage, now you see for yourselves and know that by this time the summer is near. So also you, when you see these things happening, know that the kingdom of God is near. Truly I say to you that this generation will never pass away until all things take place! Heaven and earth will pass away, but my words will never pass away.

Be Alert

"But take care for yourselves, lest your hearts are weighed down with dissipation and drunkenness and the worries of daily life, and that day come upon you suddenly like a trap. For it will come upon all who reside on the face of the whole earth. But be alert at all times, praying that you may have strength to escape all these things that are going to happen, and to stand before the Son of Man."

Discussion Questions

1. What is the warning?

   Response: The warning is to "take care of yourselves," or, as some translations say, "to watch yourselves"

(v. 34), so that the day of Christ's return doesn't sneak up on you. Everyone will experience his second coming; only a portion of the world will be ready.

2. What is the encouragement?

Response: We are encouraged to "be alert at all times" and to pray for strength—to escape all the things that will happen and to stand before the Son of Man (v. 36).

3. How does this relate to our Advent preparation?

Response: This passage (Luke 21:34–36) is part of the larger reading (Luke 21:25–36) urging those who belong to Christ to be ready for his return and looking for the signs of his return that God will reveal. In our Advent preparation, we again remember that he will come back, so we must prepare for his return.

WEEK TWO: Anticipation

Anticipation and preparation go together. If we do not anticipate that something will happen, chances are that we will not prepare for it either.

Anticipating Christ's return involves believing it will happen. It involves remembering what was foretold about him. As Christ was prophesied to come as a babe to Bethlehem (and to die upon the cross), so he is prophesied to come again to take us home.

Anticipating Christ's return prompts us to respond as John did: "Amen! Come, Lord Jesus!" (Rev 22:20).

SUNDAY: Malachi 3:1-4

> "Look! I am going to send my messenger, and he will prepare the way before me. And the Lord whom you are seeking will come suddenly to his temple, and the messenger of the covenant, in whom you are taking pleasure—look!—he is about to come," says Yahweh of hosts. And who can endure the day of his coming? And who is the one who can stand when he appears? For he is like a refiner's fire, like launderers' alkali. He will sit as a refiner and purifier of silver; he will purify the children of Levi, and he will refine them like gold and like silver, and they will present to Yahweh

offerings in righteousness. And the offering of Judah and Jerusalem will be pleasing to Yahweh, like in the days of old and like in former years.

Discussion Questions

1. What is the messenger's purpose?

   Response: The messenger prepares the way for the arrival of the Lord (v. 1).

2. What will the Lord do when he arrives?

   Response: According to verse 3, "He will purify the children of Levi, and he will refine them like gold and silver."

3. How does this relate to our anticipation of Christ's return?

   Response: As we prepare for Christ's return, we begin to anticipate and eagerly desire his return—leading us to actively prepare his way.

MONDAY: Luke 1:68-79 (Part 1)

"Blessed be the Lord, the God of Israel,
   because he has visited to help and has
   redeemed his people,

and has raised up a horn of salvation for us
    in the house of his servant David,
just as he spoke through the mouth of his holy
prophets from earliest times—
    salvation from our enemies and from the hand
    of all those who hate us,
to show mercy to our fathers
    and to remember his holy covenant,
the oath that he swore to Abraham our father,
    to grant us that we, being rescued from the
    hand of our enemies,
could serve him without fear in holiness and
righteousness
    before him all our days.
And so you, child, will be called the prophet of the
Most High,
    for you will go on before the Lord to prepare
    his ways,
to give knowledge of salvation to his people
    by the forgiveness of their sins,
because of the merciful compassion of our God
    by which the dawn will visit to help us from on
    high,
to give light to those who sit in darkness and in
the shadow of death,
    to direct our feet into the way of peace."

Discussion Questions

1. This passage is from Zechariah's praise of God for the birth of his son, John the Baptist. What was John's role in Jesus' arrival?

   Response: John the Baptist, who was also Jesus' cousin, proclaimed Jesus' arrival.

2. What does Zechariah praise God for?

   Response: Zechariah praises God that he:

   - has redeemed us (v. 68)
   - acted to save us (vv. 69–71)
   - has shown us mercy (v. 72)
   - remembers his covenant with us (v. 72)
   - reminds us to keep our end of that covenant with him (vv. 73–75)

3. How does this relate to our anticipation of Christ's return?

   Response: Zechariah's praise of God (vv. 68–75) sets the stage for the following section, where Luke introduces John the Baptist's purpose in going before the Lord. Praising God precedes the revelation of the one who will announce Christ. As we anticipate his arrival, we too should praise God for his goodness in providing a savior for his people.

TUESDAY: Luke 1:68-79 (Part 2)

"Blessed be the Lord, the God of Israel,
>   because he has visited to help and has
>   redeemed his people,
> and has raised up a horn of salvation for us
>   in the house of his servant David,
> just as he spoke through the mouth of his holy
> prophets from earliest times—
>   salvation from our enemies and from the hand
>   of all those who hate us,
> to show mercy to our fathers
>   and to remember his holy covenant,
> the oath that he swore to Abraham our father,
>   to grant us that we, being rescued from the
>   hand of our enemies,
> could serve him without fear in holiness and
> righteousness
>   before him all our days.
> And so you, child, will be called the prophet of the
> Most High,
>   for you will go on before the Lord to prepare
>   his ways,
> to give knowledge of salvation to his people
>   by the forgiveness of their sins,
> because of the merciful compassion of our God
>   by which the dawn will visit to help us from on
>   high,

to give light to those who sit in darkness and in the shadow of death,

> to direct our feet into the way of peace."

Discussion Questions

1. Who is the "child" in v. 76?

   Response: The child is John the Baptist.

2. What will the child be doing, and why?

   Response: He will be a "prophet of the Most High" (v. 76). He will "go on before the Lord" (v. 76) with these four purposes (this isn't an exclusive or exhaustive list):

   - "to prepare [the Lord's] ways" (v. 76)
   - "to give knowledge of salvation to [the Lord's] people" (v. 77)
   - "to give light to those who sit in darkness" (v. 79)
   - "to direct our feet into the way of peace" (v. 79)

   The main reason for John's role is found in v. 78: "because of the merciful compassion of our God."

3. How does this relate to our anticipation of Christ's return?

   Response: In Luke 1:68–79, Zechariah clarifies the role of John the Baptist as one of announcer and preparer.

Some of the same things that John the Baptist did to "prepare the way of the Lord" are things that we can do to prepare for and anticipate the second advent of our Lord, savior, and king.

WEDNESDAY: Philippians 1:3-11 (Part 1)

I give thanks to my God upon my every re-membrance of you, always in my every prayer for all of you, making the prayer with joy, be-cause of your participation in the gospel from the first day until now, convinced of this same thing, that the one who began a good work in you will finish it until the day of Christ Jesus, just as it is right for me to think this about all of you, because I have you in my heart, since both in my imprisonment and in the defense and confirmation of the gospel all of you are sharers of grace with me. For God is my wit-ness, that I long for all of you with the affec-tion of Christ Jesus.

And this I pray: that your love may abound still more and more in knowledge and all dis-cernment, so that you may approve what is superior, in order that you may be sincere and blameless in the day of Christ, having been filled with the fruit of righteousness which comes through Jesus Christ to the glory and praise of God.

Discussion Questions

1. What is "the day of Jesus Christ" referring to?

   Response: This speaks of the time of Christ's second coming.

2. What does it mean to be a "sharer" of grace?

   Response: Here Paul justifies his encouragement of the Philippians—one reason he "[has them] in his heart" (v. 7) is their mutual reliance on grace for their salvation.

3. How does this relate to our anticipation of Christ's return?

   Response: As we consider Christ's first advent in Bethlehem, and as we anticipate his second advent, the thought that Christ works in us through grace to save us should encourage us all the more as we look for his coming.

THURSDAY: Philippians 1:3-11 (Part 2)

I give thanks to my God upon my every remembrance of you, always in my every prayer for all of you, making the prayer with joy, because of your participation in the gospel from the first day until now, convinced of this same thing, that the one who began a good work in you will finish it until the day of Christ Jesus, just as it is right for me to think this about all of you, because I have you in my heart, since both in my imprisonment and in the defense and confirmation of the gospel all of you are sharers of grace with me. For God is my witness, that I long for all of you with the affection of Christ Jesus.

And this I pray: that your love may abound still more and more in knowledge and all discernment, so that you may approve what is superior, in order that you may be sincere and blameless in the day of Christ, having been filled with the fruit of righteousness which comes through Jesus Christ to the glory and praise of God.

Discussion Questions

1. What is Paul's prayer for the Philippians?

   Response: Paul prays that the Philippians' love may "abound" with the end result that they may "be sincere and blameless in the day of Christ" (v. 10) and also that they be "filled with the fruit of righteousness" (v. 11).

2. How does this relate to our anticipation of Christ's return?

Response: As the day of Christ approaches, this should be our prayer, too. We should desire to be blameless and pure in his sight, praising him for the grace that accomplishes this.

FRIDAY: Luke 3:1-6 (Part 1)

Now in the fifteenth year of the reign of Tiberius Caesar, when Pontius Pilate was governor of Judea, and Herod was tetrarch of Galilee, and his brother Philip was tetrarch of the region of Iturea and Trachonitis, and Lysanias was tetrarch of Abilene, in the time of the high priest Annas and Caiaphas, the word of God came to John the son of Zechariah in the wilderness. And he went into all the surrounding region of the Jordan, preaching a baptism of repentance for the forgiveness of sins, as it is written in the book of the words of the prophet Isaiah,

> "The voice of one crying out in the wilderness,
> 'Prepare the way of the Lord,
>   make his paths straight!
> Every valley will be filled,

> and every mountain and hill will be
> leveled,
> and the crooked will become straight,
>   and the rough road will become
> smooth,
> and all flesh will see the salvation of
> God.' "

Discussion Questions

1. Why are these verses—which list so many time frames, names, offices, and locations—important?

   Response: John the Baptist's ministry preparing for Christ, and Christ's life and death, are not fiction. Information like time frames, names, dates, and locations give us a historical anchor point for the events described in the Gospels.

2. How does this relate to our anticipation of Christ's return?

   Response: As the beginning of John the Baptist's ministry is not fictional, and as Christ's life, death, and resurrection are not fictional, so too his second coming is not fictional. It will happen! As partakers of his grace, we should look forward to his arrival.

SATURDAY: Luke 3:1-6 (Part 2)

Now in the fifteenth year of the reign of Tiberius Caesar, when Pontius Pilate was governor of Judea, and Herod was tetrarch of Galilee, and his brother Philip was tetrarch of the region of Iturea and Trachonitis, and Lysanias was tetrarch of Abilene, in the time of the high priest Annas and Caiaphas, the word of God came to John the son of Zechariah in the wilderness. And he went into all the surrounding region of the Jordan, preaching a baptism of repentance for the forgiveness of sins, as it is written in the book of the words of the prophet Isaiah,

> "The voice of one crying out in the wilderness,
> 'Prepare the way of the Lord,
>   make his paths straight!
> Every valley will be filled,
>   and every mountain and hill will be leveled,
> and the crooked will become straight,
>   and the rough road will become smooth,
> and all flesh will see the salvation of God.'"

Discussion Questions

1. What did John the Baptist do?

   Response: He proclaimed a baptism of repentance for the forgiveness of sins.

2. Why does the quotation from Isaiah 40:3-5 apply to John the Baptist and his work?

   Response: John the Baptist's work and preaching paved the way for Jesus. John's message is for all to prepare, because "the salvation of God" (v. 6) is coming. John's work was foretold by the prophet Isaiah, and using the passage from Isaiah to confirm John's role and work puts the focus squarely on Jesus and the salvation he brings.

3. How does this relate to our anticipation of Christ's return?

   Response: In the same way as John the Baptist announced and anticipated Jesus' ministry, we should look forward to and proclaim Christ's second coming.

WEEK THREE: Joy

Preparation and anticipation have focused our thoughts and actions on the arrival of Christ. As this arrival draws closer, a natural consequence is joy. When the thing we have been waiting for gets closer and closer, joy increases.

When I was a boy, my dad was in the Navy. There were times he was away from home for months. We wrote letters—there was no email then—to keep in touch. If he was in port, he would call us. But as the day of his homecoming drew closer, our whole family grew excited. The joy started before he came home, when months turned to weeks, weeks turned to days, and days turned to hours.

Joy is a natural part of anticipating Christ's return as we consider what he has accomplished for us and what he will accomplish for us. Our Savior lives! Our King is returning! And he will take us home.

SUNDAY: Zephaniah 3:14-20 (Part 1)

Shout for joy, O daughter of Zion!
  Cry aloud, O Israel!
Rejoice and be jubilant with all your heart,
  O daughter of Jerusalem!
Yahweh has annulled your judgments;
  he has turned away your enemies.
The king of Israel, Yahweh, is in your midst;

you shall no longer fear misfortune.
On that day it shall be said to Jerusalem,
    "Fear not, O Zion;
    your hands shall not hang limp.
Yahweh your God is in your midst;
    a mighty warrior who saves.
He shall rejoice over you with joy;
    he renews you in his love;
    he will exult over you with singing.
I will gather those of you grieving on account of
the feast;
    they were raising against her a reproach.
Behold, at that time I will deal with all your
oppressors;
    I will save the lame and gather the outcast.
I will change them from shame
    to glory and renown throughout the whole
    world.
At that time I will bring you in;
    at the time of my gathering you together.
For I will make you renowned and praised
    among all the nations of the earth
when I restore your fortunes before your eyes,"
    says Yahweh.

Discussion Questions

1. Who is the daughter of Zion/daughter of Jerusalem?

   Response: This is a poetic reference to Israel, the people of God.

2. What is the reason for her rejoicing?

   Response: There are three reasons given in verse 15, all interrelated:

   1. "Yahweh has annulled your judgments"
   2. "[Yahweh] has turned away your enemies"
   3. "The King of Israel, Yahweh, is in your midst"

   Yahweh has turned back any charge or judgment against Israel; they are no longer subject to it. Yahweh has pushed back Israel's enemies. And Yahweh is with Israel. Because of all this, Israel shall "no longer fear misfortune."

3. How does this relate to joy during the Advent season?

   Response: At the coming of the King of Israel, those who call him king have no reason to fear evil. He is in their midst, and will protect and preserve them. He has "annulled the judgments" against them (v. 15). These are reasons for joy—reminding us that our Lord will return, he has already cleansed us from our sin, and he will take us home. We will never again fear evil.

MONDAY: Zephaniah 3:14-20 (Part 2)

Shout for joy, O daughter of Zion!
    Cry aloud, O Israel!
Rejoice and be jubilant with all your heart,
    O daughter of Jerusalem!
Yahweh has annulled your judgments;
    he has turned away your enemies.
The king of Israel, Yahweh, is in your midst;
    you shall no longer fear misfortune.
On that day it shall be said to Jerusalem,
    "Fear not, O Zion;
    your hands shall not hang limp.
Yahweh your God is in your midst;
    a mighty warrior who saves.
He shall rejoice over you with joy;
    he renews you in his love;
    he will exult over you with singing.
I will gather those of you grieving on account of
the feast;
    they were raising against her a reproach.
Behold, at that time I will deal with all your
oppressors;
    I will save the lame and gather the outcast.
I will change them from shame
    to glory and renown throughout the whole
    world.
At that time I will bring you in;
    at the time of my gathering you together.

For I will make you renowned and praised
    among all the nations of the earth
when I restore your fortunes before your eyes,"
    says Yahweh.

Discussion Questions

1. What does this passage say about the Lord?

   Response: This passage (v. 17) says that:

   - The Lord is mighty and will save us
   - He will rejoice over us
   - His love will renew us

2. How does this relate to joy during the Advent season?

   Response: The Lord is coming back to save us, and he will rejoice for our salvation. This should encourage our joy at the thought of his return.

TUESDAY: Zephaniah 3:14-20 (Part 3)

Shout for joy, O daughter of Zion!
    Cry aloud, O Israel!
Rejoice and be jubilant with all your heart,
    O daughter of Jerusalem!
Yahweh has annulled your judgments;
    he has turned away your enemies.
The king of Israel, Yahweh, is in your midst;

you shall no longer fear misfortune.
On that day it shall be said to Jerusalem,
 "Fear not, O Zion;
 your hands shall not hang limp.
Yahweh your God is in your midst;
 a mighty warrior who saves.
He shall rejoice over you with joy;
 he renews you in his love;
 he will exult over you with singing.
I will gather those of you grieving on account of
the feast;
 they were raising against her a reproach.
Behold, at that time I will deal with all your
oppressors;
 I will save the lame and gather the outcast.
I will change them from shame
 to glory and renown throughout the whole
 world.
At that time I will bring you in;
 at the time of my gathering you together.
For I will make you renowned and praised
 among all the nations of the earth
when I restore your fortunes before your eyes,"
 says Yahweh.

Discussion Questions

1. What will the Lord do upon his return (v. 19)?

   Response: Those who oppress others will be dealt with by Yahweh. Those who are lame will be healed. Those who are the Lord's will be "renowned and praised among all the nations of the earth."

2. How does this relate to joy during the Advent season?

   Response: Not only is the Lord coming back, he will establish his kingdom and restore his people. His people will be known among all the nations, and their fortunes will be restored. This knowledge should give us joy!

WEDNESDAY: Isaiah 12:2-6

Look! God is my salvation;
    I will trust, and I will not be afraid,
for my strength and might is Yah, Yahweh;
    and he has become salvation for me."

And you will draw water from the wells of
salvation in joy. And you will say on that day,

"Give thanks to Yahweh;
    call on his name.
Make his deeds known among the peoples;
    bring to remembrance that his name is exalted.

Sing praises to Yahweh, for he has done a glorious
thing;
　　this is known in all the earth.
Inhabitant of Zion, shout out and sing for joy,
　　for the holy one of Israel is great in your midst."

Discussion Questions

1. How is God portrayed?

Response: God is salvation, and he is worthy of all
trust. Note how verse 2 emphasizes this concept: it
starts and ends by proclaiming God as "my salvation."

2. What is the response to God?

Response: The people are to give thanks to God, proclaim his work and name (v. 4), and sing praises to him
(v. 5).

3. How does this relate to joy during the Advent season?

Response: As Advent reminds us of the imminence
of Christ's return, our response to his return should
be the same: We should thank God, proclaim his work
and name, and sing his praises—all with joy.

THURSDAY: Philippians 4:4-7

Rejoice in the Lord always; again I say, rejoice. Let your gentleness be made known to

all people. The Lord is near. Be anxious for nothing, but in everything by prayer and supplication with thanksgiving let your requests be made known to God. And the peace of God that surpasses all understanding will guard your hearts and your minds in Christ Jesus.

Discussion Questions

1. What is commanded in these verses?

   Response: First, Paul commands the Philippians to always "rejoice in the Lord," and then he reiterates the same command: "Again I say, rejoice" (v. 4). He urges the Philippians to show gentleness (in some translations, "reasonableness") to everyone. He reminds them that the Lord is near, and because of this, to rely on God for peace (v. 6–7).

2. How does this relate to joy during the Advent season?

   Response: Advent reminds us that Christ came once, and he will come again. This is a joyous reminder, and we should rejoice!

FRIDAY: Luke 3:7-18 (Part 1)

Therefore he was saying to the crowds that came out to be baptized by him, "Offspring of vipers! Who warned you to flee from the coming wrath? Therefore produce fruit worthy of repentance! And do not begin to say to yourselves, 'We have Abraham as father.' For I say to you that God is able to raise up children for Abraham from these stones! And even now the ax is positioned at the root of the trees; therefore every tree not producing good fruit is cut down and thrown into the fire."

And the crowds were asking him, saying, "What then should we do?" And he answered and said to them, "The one who has two tunics must share with the one who does not have one, and the one who has food must do likewise." And tax collectors also came to be baptized, and they said to him, "Teacher, what should we do?" And he said to them, "Collect no more than what you are ordered to." And those who served in the army were also asking him, saying, "What should we also do?" And he said to them, "Extort from no one, and do not blackmail anyone, and be content with your pay."

And while the people were waiting expectantly and all were pondering in their hearts concerning John, whether perhaps he might be the Christ, John answered them all, saying, "I baptize you with water, but the one who is more powerful than I am is coming, of whom I am not worthy to untie the strap of his sandals.

He will baptize you with the Holy Spirit and fire. His winnowing shovel is in his hand, to clean out his threshing floor and to gather the wheat into his storehouse, but he will burn up the chaff with unquenchable fire."

So with many other exhortations also he proclaimed good news to the people.

Discussion Questions

1. What sorts of things was John the Baptist telling the crowds that came to see him and be baptized by him?

   Response: John urges them to "produce fruit worthy of repentance" (v. 8). Further, he tells them to share what they have (v. 11); he tells the tax collectors to only collect what they are authorized to collect (v. 13) and urges soldiers to be content with their wages (v. 14).

2. Verse 15 starts, "And while the people were waiting expectantly." Are you in expectation?

   Response: Think and reflect on this question, whether on your own or in a group.

3. How does this relate to joy during the Advent season?

   Response: Advent reminds us that our expectation of Christ's return is, with every passing day, closer to becoming our present reality.

SATURDAY: Luke 3:7-18 (Part 2)

Therefore he was saying to the crowds that came out to be baptized by him, "Offspring of vipers! Who warned you to flee from the coming wrath? Therefore produce fruit worthy of repentance! And do not begin to say to yourselves, 'We have Abraham as father.' For I say to you that God is able to raise up children for Abraham from these stones! And even now the ax is positioned at the root of the trees; therefore every tree not producing good fruit is cut down and thrown into the fire."

And the crowds were asking him, saying, "What then should we do?" And he answered and said to them, "The one who has two tunics must share with the one who does not have one, and the one who has food must do likewise." And tax collectors also came to be baptized, and they said to him, "Teacher, what should we do?" And he said to them, "Collect no more than what you are ordered to." And those who served in the army were also asking him, saying, "What should we also do?" And he said to them, "Extort from no one, and do not blackmail anyone, and be content with your pay."

And while the people were waiting expectantly and all were pondering in their hearts concerning John, whether perhaps he might be the Christ, John answered them all, saying, "I baptize you with water, but the one who is more powerful than I am is coming, of whom I am not worthy to untie the strap of his sandals. He will baptize you with the Holy Spirit and fire. His winnowing shovel is in his hand, to clean out his threshing floor and to gather the wheat into his storehouse, but he will burn up the chaff with unquenchable fire."

So with many other exhortations also he proclaimed good news to the people.

Discussion Questions

1. How did John the Baptist respond to those wondering if he was the Christ (the Messiah)?

   Response: John makes it plain that the Christ is greater than he is (v. 16–17).

2. What will the Christ do when he comes?

   Response: The Christ will baptize with the Holy Spirit and with fire. He also will gather up his own (the wheat), but he will burn those who are not his (the chaff) "with unquenchable fire" (v. 17).

3. How does this relate to joy during the Advent season?

   Response: Christ will return, will gather us up, and make us his. This is cause for rejoicing!

WEEK FOUR: Incarnation

Incarnation is a mysterious thing that we cannot fully comprehend: How the Son of the living God took on flesh to be like us, to save us. Though we do not understand how it happened, we can, like the author of Hebrews, appreciate it greatly:

> Therefore, since the children share in blood and flesh, he also in like manner shared in these same things, in order that through death he could destroy the one who has the power of death, that is, the devil, and could set free these who through fear of death were subject to slavery throughout all their lives. For surely he is not concerned with angels, but he is concerned with the descendants of Abraham. Therefore he was obligated to be made like his brothers in all respects, in order that he could become a merciful and faithful high priest in the things relating to God, in order to make atonement for the sins of the people. For in that which he himself suffered when he was tempted, he is able to help those who are tempted (Hebrews 2:14–18).

SUNDAY: Micah 5:2-5

But you, O Bethlehem Ephrathah,
    too small to be among the clans of Judah,
from you one will go out for me,
    to be ruler in Israel;
and his origins are from of old,
    from ancient days.
Therefore he will give them up
    until the time of she who is with child has
    given birth.
And the rest of his brothers will return
    to the children of Israel.
And he will stand and shepherd his flock
    in the strength of Yahweh,
    in the majesty of the name of Yahweh his God.
And they will live,
    for now he will be great unto the ends of the
    earth.
And this one will be peace.
As for the Assyrian, when he comes into our land
    and when he treads on our fortresses,
then we will raise up against him seven shepherds
    and eight leaders of men.

Discussion Questions

1. What does the word "incarnation" mean?

   Response: "Incarnate" means to be made into flesh. It is used to express how Jesus—who is fully divine—could take on flesh and become human.

2. How does this passage relate to the incarnation of Jesus?

   Response: This passage speaks of when "she who is with child has given birth" (v. 3). We know that the one that Israel awaits was prophesied to be born of a woman. The Gospel of Matthew also uses part of this prophecy (see Matthew 2:6) and applies it to Jesus.

3. How does this passage show that the incarnation is important to remember during Advent?

   Response: The one who will be born of a woman will come to be ruler and to set his people free. He will "shepherd his flock in the strength of Yahweh" (v. 4), and they will dwell securely—he shall be their peace.

MONDAY: Psalm 96

> Sing to Yahweh a new song;
> sing to Yahweh, all the earth.
> Sing to Yahweh; bless his name.
> Announce his salvation from day to day.

Tell his glory among the nations,
his marvelous works among all the peoples.
For Yahweh is great and very worthy of praise;
he is to be feared above all gods.
For all the gods of the peoples are idols,
but Yahweh made the heavens.
Splendor and majesty are before him;
strength and beauty are in his sanctuary.
Ascribe to Yahweh, you families of the peoples,
ascribe to Yahweh glory and strength.
Ascribe to Yahweh the glory due his name;
bring an offering and come into his courts.
Worship Yahweh in holy array;
tremble before him, all the earth.
Say among the nations, "Yahweh is king!
Yes, the world is established so that it will not be
moved.
He will judge the peoples fairly."
Let the heavens be glad and the earth rejoice.
Let the sea with its fullness roar.
Let the field with all that is in it exult.
Then all the trees of the forests will sing for joy
before Yahweh, for he is coming;
for he is coming to judge the earth.
He will judge the world with righteousness,
and the peoples with his faithfulness.

Discussion Questions

1. What are some qualities of Yahweh mentioned in this psalm?

   Response: Yahweh's attributes include:

   - He is "great and very worthy of praise" (v. 4)
   - He is "feared above all gods" (v. 4)
   - He "made the heavens" (v. 5)
   - He has splendor, majesty, strength, and beauty (v. 6)
   - He has glory and strength (vv. 7–8)
   - The fields and forests will rejoice and sing for him (v. 12)
   - He will judge the world and the peoples (v. 13)

2. How does this passage show that the incarnation is important to remember during Advent?

   Response: Because he is the Lord, and he has saved us. We are his people. The greatness of his work in saving us, in providing Jesus Christ as our atoning sacrifice, is reason for praise.

TUESDAY: Hebrews 10:5-10

Therefore, when he came into the world, he
said,

> "Sacrifice and offering you did not want,
>> but a body you prepared for me;
> you did not delight in whole burnt
> offerings and offerings for sins.
>> Then I said, 'Behold, I have come—
> in the roll of the book it is written about
> me—
>> to do your will, O God.'"

When he says above,

> "Sacrifices and offerings and whole
> burnt offerings and offerings for sin
>> you did not want, nor did you
> delight in,"

which are offered according to the law, then
he has said,

> "Behold, I have come to do your will."

He takes away the first in order to establish
the second, by which will we are made holy
through the offering of the body of Jesus
Christ once for all.

Discussion Questions

1. What was the effect of sacrifices and offerings?

   Response: While useful for the purposes for which God established them, sacrifices and offerings made according to the law ultimately weren't pleasing to God (v. 6). To permanently achieve their purpose (appeasing God's wrath due to our sin), something else had to be done.

2. What is the effect of the "offering of the body of Jesus Christ" (v. 10)?

   Response: The offering of Jesus Christ is effective "once for all" (v. 10). It achieves what sacrifices and offerings under the law could not accomplish: our sanctification.

3. How does this passage show that the incarnation is important to remember during Advent?

   Response: Note that sanctification happens "through the offering of the body of Jesus Christ" (v. 10). The human body of Jesus Christ—the fact that he was fully human and, of course, fully God—plays a necessary role in our sanctification. Without the human body and nature of Christ, this would not have been accomplished. The incarnation is, indeed, important!

WEDNESDAY: Titus 2:11-14

> For the grace of God has appeared, bringing salvation to all people, training us in order that, denying impiety and worldly desires, we may live self-controlled and righteously and godly in the present age, looking forward to the blessed hope and the glorious appearing of our great God and Savior Jesus Christ, who gave himself for us, in order that he might redeem us from all lawlessness and purify for himself a people for his own possession, zealous for good deeds.

Discussion Questions

1. In this passage, "the grace of God" (v. 11) is personified. He appears and brings salvation. Who is this figure?

   Response: "The grace of God" is the one who brings the grace and the one who enables us to receive grace: Jesus Christ.

2. What does he ("the grace of God") "train" us to do?

   Response: The passage mentions three things:

   - To deny impiety (ungodliness) and worldly passions (v. 12)
   - To live self-controlled, righteous, and godly lives in the present age (v. 12)

- To anticipate the appearing of the glory of our great God and savior, Jesus Christ (v. 13)

3. How does this passage show that the incarnation is important to remember during Advent?

Response: Because of the incarnation, we are redeemed, and we are "his own possession" (v. 14).

THURSDAY: Titus 3:4-7

> But when the kindness and love for mankind of God our Savior appeared, he saved us, not by deeds of righteousness that we have done, but because of his mercy, through the washing of regeneration and renewal by the Holy Spirit, whom he poured out on us abundantly through Jesus Christ our Savior, so that, having been justified by his grace, we may become heirs according to the hope of eternal life.

Discussion Questions

1. Who is "the kindness and love for mankind of God our Savior"?

Response: The same as "the grace of God who appeared" in Titus 2:11—Jesus Christ.

2. What did he ("the kindness and love for mankind of God our Savior") do, and why did he do it?

   Response: He saved us. And he did it not because of anything righteous that we did, but because of his mercy (see also Eph 2:6–8).

3. How did he do it?

   Response: He saved us "through the washing of regeneration and renewal of the Holy Spirit" (v. 5), whom we have because of Jesus Christ. Because of this we are justified, and we have the sure hope of eternal life.

4. How does this passage show that the incarnation is important to remember during Advent?

   Response: Jesus Christ, God incarnate, is our savior. Without him, we have no hope of eternal life. With him, we are "heirs according to the hope of eternal life." We should cherish this!

FRIDAY: Luke 1:39-55 (Part 1)

> Now in those days Mary set out and traveled with haste into the hill country, to a town of Judah, and entered into the house of Zechariah, and greeted Elizabeth. And it happened that when Elizabeth heard the greeting of Mary, the baby in her womb leaped and Elizabeth

was filled with the Holy Spirit. And she cried out with a loud shout and said,

> "Blessed are you among women,
>   and blessed is the fruit of your womb!

And why is this granted to me, that the mother of my Lord should come to me? For behold, when the sound of your greeting came to my ears, the baby in my womb leaped for joy! And blessed is she who believed that there will be a fulfillment to what was spoken to her from the Lord!"

And Mary said,

> "My soul exalts the Lord,
>   and my spirit has rejoiced greatly in God my Savior,
>   because he has looked upon the humble state of his female slave,
>   for behold, from now on all generations will consider me blessed,
>   because the Mighty One has done great things for me,
>   and holy is his name.
>   And his mercy is for generation after generation
>   to those who fear him.
>   He has done a mighty deed with his arm;

he has dispersed the proud in the
thoughts of their hearts.

He has brought down rulers from
their thrones,

and has exalted the lowly.

He has filled those who are hungry
with good things,

and those who are rich he has sent
away empty-handed.

He has helped Israel his servant,

remembering his mercy,

just as he spoke to our fathers,

to Abraham and to his descendants
forever."

Discussion Questions

1. How does this passage show that Jesus Christ was
   incarnate?

   Response: Mary is referred to as "mother of my Lord"
   (v. 43). In Luke's account, this happens after the angel
   has visited Mary to tell her about Jesus.

2. How does this passage show that the incarnation is
   important to remember during Advent?

   Response: The baby in Elizabeth's womb—John the
   Baptist—jumped at Mary's presence. Elizabeth is
   filled with the Holy Spirit and pronounces a blessing

on Mary, the mother of Jesus. The incarnation was precious to Elizabeth; we should treasure it, too.

SATURDAY: Luke 1:39-55 (Part 2)

Now in those days Mary set out and traveled with haste into the hill country, to a town of Judah, and entered into the house of Zechariah, and greeted Elizabeth. And it happened that when Elizabeth heard the greeting of Mary, the baby in her womb leaped and Elizabeth was filled with the Holy Spirit. And she cried out with a loud shout and said,

> "Blessed are you among women,
>> and blessed is the fruit of your womb!

And why is this granted to me, that the mother of my Lord should come to me? For behold, when the sound of your greeting came to my ears, the baby in my womb leaped for joy! And blessed is she who believed that there will be a fulfillment to what was spoken to her from the Lord!"

And Mary said,

> "My soul exalts the Lord,
>> and my spirit has rejoiced greatly in God my Savior,

because he has looked upon the humble state of his female slave,

for behold, from now on all generations will consider me blessed,

because the Mighty One has done great things for me,

and holy is his name.

And his mercy is for generation after generation

to those who fear him.

He has done a mighty deed with his arm;

he has dispersed the proud in the thoughts of their hearts.

He has brought down rulers from their thrones,

and has exalted the lowly.

He has filled those who are hungry with good things,

and those who are rich he has sent away empty-handed.

He has helped Israel his servant,

remembering his mercy,

just as he spoke to our fathers,

to Abraham and to his descendants forever."

Discussion Questions

1. This is Mary's response to Elizabeth's blessing. It is also known as the "Magnificat" (which is the first word of Mary's response in the Latin translation of the Bible). What is Mary's response?

   Response: "My soul exalts the Lord" (v. 46). Mary's response is to exalt the Lord—to praise him.

2. How does this passage show that the incarnation is important to remember during Advent?

   Response: Mary notes that future generations will call her "blessed" as a result of her role in the incarnation of Christ.

READINGS FOR
Christmas Eve and Christmas Day

CHRISTMAS EVE: Isaiah 9:2-7

The people who walked in darkness have seen a
great light;
> light has shined on those who lived in a land of
> darkness.

You have made the nation numerous;
> you have not made the joy great.

They rejoice in your presence as *with* joy at the
harvest,
> as they rejoice when they divide plunder.

For you have shattered the yoke of its burden
> and the stick of its shoulder,
> the rod of its oppressor, on the day of Midian.

For every boot that marches and shakes the earth
> and garment rolled in blood

will be for burning—fire fuel.

For a child has been born for us;
> a son has been given to us.

And the dominion will be on his shoulder,
> and his name is called Wonderful Counselor,
> Mighty God,
> Everlasting Father, Prince of Peace.

His dominion will grow continually,
 and to peace there will be no end
on the throne of David and over his kingdom,
 to establish it and sustain it
with justice and righteousness
 now and forever.
The zeal of Yahweh of hosts will do this.

Discussion Questions

1. Isaiah 9:6–7 is often read at Christmas. What do verses 2–5 add to our understanding of the whole passage?

   Response: Verse 2 contrasts darkness and light to introduce the light. Verse 3 introduces the joy this light brings. Verses 4 and 5 recall trouble and cast the light as the solution to the trouble. Into this, verse 6 explains the light, the child that is to come.

2. How does this passage show that the incarnation is important to remember during Advent?

   Response: The one who brings the light; the one who brings the joy; the one who is the solution to present troubles—this one comes born of a woman. The one who saves us was born of a woman and was human himself. During Advent we remember his first arrival and look forward to his second coming.

CHRISTMAS DAY: Luke 2:1-20

Now it happened that in those days a decree went out from Caesar Augustus to register all the empire. (This first registration took place when Quirinius was governor of Syria.) And everyone went to be registered, each one to his own town. So Joseph also went up from Galilee, from the town of Nazareth, to Judea, to the city of David which is called Bethlehem, because he was of the house and family line of David, to be registered together with Mary, who was legally promised in marriage to him and was pregnant. And it happened that while they were there, the time came for her to give birth. And she gave birth to her firstborn son, and wrapped him in strips of cloth and laid him in a manger, because there was no place for them in the inn.

And there were shepherds in the same region, living out of doors and keeping watch, guarding over their flock by night. And an angel of the Lord stood near them, and the glory of the Lord shone around them, and they were terribly frightened. And the angel said to them, "Do not be afraid, for behold, I bring good news to you of great joy which will be for all the people: that today a Savior, who is Christ the Lord, was born for you in the city of David. And this will be the sign for you: you will find the baby wrapped in strips of cloth and lying in a manger." And suddenly there was with the angel a multitude of the heavenly army, praising God and saying,

> "Glory to God in the highest,
>> and on earth peace
>> among people with whom he is
> pleased!"

And it happened that when the angels had departed from them into heaven, the shepherds began to say to one another, "Let us go now to Bethlehem and see this thing that has happened, which the Lord has revealed to us!" And they went hurrying and found both Mary and Joseph, and the baby who was lying in the manger. And when they saw it, they made known the statement that had been told to them about this child. And all who heard it were astonished concerning what had been said to them by the shepherds. But Mary treasured up all these words, pondering them in her heart. And the shepherds returned, glorifying and praising God for all that they had heard and seen, just as it had been told to them.

Discussion Questions

1. Jesus Christ, the Messiah, our Savior, was born into the world as a baby. What was the reaction of those who witnessed this event?

   Response: The angel who appeared to the shepherds announcing the birth was quickly joined by a multitude that praised God in a magnificent way. Mary "treasured up all these words, pondering them in her heart" (v. 19). This refers to the story of the shepherds and the angels' praise. And the shepherds reacted much the same as the angels, "glorifying and praising God," because what they had heard and seen was as it had been told to them.

2. What should our reaction to the birth of our Savior be this Christmas Day?

   Response: The shepherds are our model: They heard, they saw, and they glorified and praised God. As we remember his birth (and we anticipate his second coming), let us praise and glorify God for his magnificent salvation!